Prayers That Avail Much®
for the Workplace

The Business Handbook of Scriptural Prayer

James 5:16

by
Germaine Copeland

And this is the confidence that we have in him, that, if we ask any thing according to his will, he heareth us: and if we know that he hear us, whatsoever we ask, we know that we have the petitions that we desired of him.

1 John 5:14,15

Harrison House
Tulsa, Oklahoma

Prayers That Avail Much® *for the Workplace*
ISBN 1-57794-349-X
Copyright © 2001 by Germaine Copeland

Germaine Copeland, President
Word Ministries, Inc.
38 Sloan Street
Roswell, Georgia 30075
www.prayers.org

Published by Harrison House, Inc.
P.O. Box 35035
Tulsa, Oklahoma 74153

Contents

Preface

When I was first asked by my publisher, Keith Provance, to write a prayer book for business professionals, I thought it was a good idea, but I felt that the prayers in my other books were already inclusive of all business purposes. Relentlessly, Keith persisted, and God reinforced His plan and design for Word Ministries—to write scriptural prayers for everyday living.

There is unlimited power in prayers that avail much (James 5:16 AMP).

In the Scriptures, success is guaranteed in the person who gives Jesus preeminence in the world of business: **And he is the head of the body, the church: who is the beginning, the firstborn from the dead; that in *all things* he might have the preeminence. For it pleased the Father that in him should *all* fullness dwell** (Col. 1:18,19).

My husband and I start each morning by giving thanks to God for the beginning of another day, acknowledging Jesus as Lord and praying for godly wisdom in every decision. We ask the Lord to make us a blessing to others and to give us favor and understanding in our respective places of business.

Honor God and give Him glory for your success: **…remember the Lord your God, for it is he who gives you the ability to produce wealth, and so confirms his covenant, which he swore to your forefathers, as it is today** (Deut. 8:18 NIV). Pray on every occasion, asking for godly wisdom without misgiving or reservation: **If any of you lacks wisdom, he should ask God, who gives generously to all without finding fault, and it will be given to him** (James 1:5 NIV).

Prayer will bring personal changes in you and will produce conduct in you that will ensure your success in life.

Jesus said of those who put their trust in Him, **…I have come that they may have life, and have it to the full** (John 10:10 NIV). Financial success alone is not our standard, but Jesus Himself is our Guide for victorious living at home and at work.

Define your identity, your integrity and your influence by praying powerful prayers that avail much.

Acknowledgments

It is always my desire to give honor where honor is due (Rom. 13:7). I thank my Father God for the inter-cessors here at Word Ministries and for other prayer partners who have faithfully prayed for me and the development of this work. I appreciate their support and encouragement: **Except the Lord builds the house, they labor in vain who build it...** (Ps. 127:1 AMP).

In writing this book, I collaborated with a corpo-ration CEO who is committed totally to ministry and to the service of our God, seeking to bring honor and glory to the name of Jesus. He has contributed heart-felt prayers which have proven invaluable in his personal pursuit of triumphant living and his success in business. I express my appreciation for his making this knowledge widely available to others through his contribution to this book.

A special thank you goes to Donna Walker, my friend and editor, who continues to assist me in writing prayers that avail much. The Holy Spirit is our

Guide through countless hours of praying, writing, editing and rewriting.

Jan Duncan, a business administrator for Word Ministries, deserves acknowledgment for her faith in the global vision of this ministry. Her years of experience in the secular business world prepared her "for such a time as this" (Esth. 4:14). She encourages me to develop God-given leadership abilities and proficient business acumen, assuring me that He Who called is utterly faithful and He will finish what He has set out to do (1 Thess. 5:24 PHILLIPS). I would be remiss without expressing my appreciation to Michal Taylor, editorial development manager, and the editorial staff at Harrison House. Thank you for all your hard work, patience and understanding.

Last, but not least, I wish to express my gratitude to Everette, my husband of forty-five years. He is a man of integrity whose private and public lifestyle is an expression of God-centered principles and sound business ethics. He has been my counselor and advisor throughout the months of writing and rewriting this book.

How To Pray Prayers That Avail Much

The prayers in the book are to be used by you for yourself and for others. They are a matter of the heart. Deliberately pray and meditate on each prayer. Allow the Holy Spirit to make the Word a reality in your heart. Your spirit will become alive to God's Word, and you will begin to think like God thinks and talk like He talks. You will find yourself poring over His Word, hungering for more and more. The Father rewards those who diligently seek Him (Heb. 11:6).

Research and contemplate the spiritual significance of each verse listed with the prayers. These are by no means the only Scriptures on certain subjects, but they are a beginning.

These prayers are a guide for you to have a more intimate relationship with your heavenly Father. The study of His Word transforms your mind and lifestyle. Then others will know that it is possible to change, and you will give hope to those who come to you seeking advice. When you admonish someone with the

Word, you are offering spiritual guidance and consolation.

Walk in God's counsel, and prize His wisdom (Ps. 1; Prov. 4:7,8). People are looking for something on which they can depend. When someone in need comes to you, you can point him to that portion in God's Word that is the answer to his problem. You become victorious, trustworthy and the one with the answer, for your heart is fixed and established on His Word (Ps. 112).

Once you begin delving into God's Word, you must commit to ordering your conversation aright (Ps. 50:23). That is being a doer of the Word. Faith always has a good report. You cannot pray effectively for yourself, for someone else or about something and then talk negatively about the matter (Matt. 12:34-37). This is being double-minded, and a double-minded man receives *nothing* from God (James 1:6-8).

In Ephesians 4:29-30 AMP it is written:

Let no foul or polluting language, nor evil word, nor unwholesome or worthless talk [ever] come out of your mouth; but only such [speech] as is good and beneficial to the spiritual progress of others, as is fitting to the need and the occasion, that it may be a blessing and give grace (God's favor) to those who hear it.

And do not grieve the Holy Spirit of God, (do not offend, or vex, or sadden Him) by whom you were sealed (marked, branded as God's own, secured) for the day of redemption—of final deliverance through Christ from evil and the consequences of sin.

Reflect on these words and give them time to keep your perspective in line with God's will. Our Father has much, so very much, to say about that little member, the tongue (James 3). Give the devil no opportunity by getting into worry, unforgiveness, strife and criticism. Put a stop to idle and foolish talking (Eph. 4:27; 5:4). You are to be a blessing to others (Gal. 6:10).

Talk the answer, not the problem. The answer is in God's Word. You must have knowledge of that Word—revelation knowledge (1 Cor. 2:7-16). The Holy Spirit, your Teacher, will reveal the things that have been freely given to us by God (John 14:26).

As an intercessor, unite with others in prayer. United prayer is a mighty weapon that the Body of Christ is to use.

Have the faith of God, and approach Him confidently. When you pray according to His will, He hears you. Then you know you have what you ask of Him (1 John 5:14-15 NIV). Do not throw away your confidence. It will be richly rewarded (Heb. 10:35 NIV). Allow your spirit to pray by the Holy Spirit. Praise God for the victory now before any manifestation. *Walk by faith and not by sight* (2 Cor. 5:7).

When your faith comes under pressure, don't be moved. As Satan attempts to challenge you, resist him steadfast in the faith—letting patience have her perfect work (James 1:4). Take the sword of the Spirit and the shield of faith and quench his every fiery dart (Eph.

6:16,17). The entire substitutionary work of Christ was for you. Satan is now a defeated foe because Jesus conquered him (Col. 2:14,15). Satan is overcome by the blood of the Lamb and the word of our testimony (Rev. 12:11). Fight the good fight of faith (1 Tim. 6:12). Withstand the adversary and be firm in faith against his onset—rooted, established, strong and determined (1 Peter 5:9). Speak God's Word boldly and courageously.

Your desire should be to please and to bless the Father. As you pray according to His Word, He joyfully hears that you—His child—are living and walking in the truth (3 John 4).

How exciting to know that the prayers of the saints are forever in the throne room (Rev. 5:8). Hallelujah!

Praise God for His Word and the limitlessness of prayer in the name of Jesus. It belongs to every child of God. Therefore, run with patience the race that is set before you, looking unto Jesus, the author and finisher of your faith (Heb. 12:1,2). God's Word is able to build you up and give you your rightful inheritance among all God's set apart ones (Acts 20:32).

Commit yourself to pray and to pray correctly by approaching the throne with your mouth filled with His Word.

Effectual Prayer

> **...The earnest (heart-felt, continued) prayer of a righteous man makes tremendous power available—dynamic in its working.**
>
> **James 5:16 AMP**

Prayer is fellowshipping with the Father—a vital, personal contact with God, Who is more than enough. We are to be in constant communion with Him:

> **For the eyes of the Lord are upon the righteous—those who are upright and in right standing with God—and His ears are attentive (open) to their prayer...**
>
> **1 Peter 3:12 AMP**

Prayer is not to be a religious form with no power. It is to be effective and accurate and bring results. God watches over His Word to perform it (Jer. 1:12).

Prayer that brings results must be based on God's Word.

> For the Word that God speaks is alive and
> full of power—making it active, operative, ener-
> gizing and effective; it is sharper than any two-
> edged sword, penetrating to the dividing line of
> the breath of life (soul) and [the immortal]
> spirit, and of joints and marrow [that is, of the
> deepest parts of our nature] exposing and sifting
> and analyzing and judging the very thoughts
> and purposes of the heart.
>
> Hebrews 4:12 AMP

Prayer is this "living" Word in our mouths. Our
mouths must speak forth faith, for faith is what pleases
God (Heb. 11:6). We hold His Word up to Him in
prayer, and our Father sees Himself in His Word.

God's Word is our contact with Him. We put
Him in remembrance of His Word (Isa. 43:26) asking
Him for what we need in the name of our Lord Jesus.
The woman in Mark 5:25-34 placed a demand on the
power of God when she said, "If I can but touch the
hem of his garmet I will be healed." By faith she
touched His clothes and was healed. We remind Him

that He supplies all of our needs according to His riches in glory by Christ Jesus (Phil. 4:19). That Word does not return to Him void—without producing any effect, useless—but it *shall* accomplish that which He pleases and purposes, and it shall prosper in the thing for which He sent it (Isa. 55:11). Hallelujah!

God did *not* leave us without His thoughts and His ways, for we have His Word—His bond. God instructs us to call Him, and He will answer and show us great and mighty things (Jer. 33:3). Prayer is to be exciting—not drudgery.

It takes someone to pray. God moves as we pray in faith—believing. He says that His eyes run to and fro throughout the whole earth to show Himself strong in behalf of those whose hearts are blameless toward Him (2 Chron. 16:9). We are blameless (Eph. 1:4). We are His very own children (Eph. 1:5). We are His righteousness in Christ Jesus (2 Cor. 5:21). He tells us to come boldly to the throne of grace and obtain mercy and find grace to help in time of need—appropriate and well-timed help (Heb. 4:16). Praise the Lord!

The prayer armor is for every believer, every member of the Body of Christ, who will put it on and walk in it, for the weapons of our warfare are not carnal but mighty through God for the pulling down of the strongholds of the enemy (Satan, the god of this world, and all his demonic forces) (2 Cor. 10:4; Eph. 6:12,18).

There are many different kinds of prayer, such as the prayer of thanksgiving and praise, the prayer of dedication and worship and the prayer that changes things (not God). All prayer involves a time of fellow-shipping with the Father.

In Ephesians 6, we are instructed to take the sword of the Spirit, which is the Word of God, and **pray at all times—on every occasion, in every season—in the Spirit, with all [manner of] prayer and entreaty** (Eph. 6:18 AMP).

In 1 Timothy 2 we are admonished and urged that **petitions, prayers, intercessions and thanksgivings be offered on behalf of all men** (1 Tim. 2:1 AMP). *Prayer is our responsibility.*

Prayer must be the foundation of every Christian endeavor. Any failure is a prayer failure. We are not to be ignorant concerning God's Word. God desires for His people to be successful, to be filled with a full, deep and clear knowledge of His will (His Word) and to bear fruit in every good work (Col. 1:9-13). We then bring honor and glory to Him (John 15:8). He desires that we know how to pray, for **the prayer of the upright is his delight** (Prov. 15:8).

Our Father has not left us helpless. Not only has He given us His Word, but also He has given us the Holy Spirit to help our infirmities when we know not how to pray as we ought (Rom. 8:26). Praise God! Our Father has provided His people with every pos-sible avenue to ensure their complete and total victory in this life in the name of our Lord Jesus (1 John 5:3-5).

We pray to the Father, in the name of Jesus, through the Holy Spirit, according to the Word!

Using God's Word on purpose, specifically, in prayer is one means of prayer, and it is a most effective and accurate means. Jesus said, **The words (truths)**

that I have been speaking to you are spirit and life
(John 6:63 AMP).

When Jesus faced Satan in the wilderness, He
said, "It is written…it is written…it is written." We are
to live, be upheld and be sustained by every word that
proceeds from the mouth of God (Matt. 4:4).

James, by the Spirit, admonishes us that we do
not have, because we do not ask. We ask and receive
not, because we ask amiss (James 4:2,3). We must heed
that admonishment now, for we are to become experts
in prayer, rightly dividing the Word of Truth (2 Tim.
2:15).

Using the Word in prayer is not taking it out of
context, for His Word in us is the key to answered
prayer—to prayer that brings results. He is able to do
exceedingly abundantly above all we ask or think,
according to the power that works in us (Eph. 3:20).
The power lies within God's Word. It is anointed by
the Word, for the Word is of the Spirit of God. We
apply that Word personally to ourselves and to others—
not adding to or taking from it—in the name of Jesus.

We apply the Word to the *now*—to those things, circumstances and situations facing each of us *now*.

Paul was very specific and definite in his praying. The first chapters of Ephesians, Philippians, Colossians and 2 Thessalonians are examples of how Paul prayed for believers. There are numerous others. *Search them out.* Paul wrote under the inspiration of the Holy Spirit. We can use these Spirit-given prayers today!

In 2 Corinthians 1:11, 2 Corinthians 9:14 and Philippians 1:4, we see examples of how believers prayed one for another—putting others first in their prayer life with joy. Our faith does work by love (Gal. 5:6). We grow spiritually as we reach out to help others—praying for and with them and holding out to them the Word of Life (Phil. 2:16).

Man is spirit, he has a soul and he lives in a body (1 Thess. 5:23). In order to operate successfully, each of these three parts must be fed properly. The soul, or intellect, feeds on intellectual food to produce intellectual strength. The body feeds on physical food to produce physical strength. The spirit—the heart or inward man—is the real you, the part that has been reborn in Christ Jesus. It must feed on spirit food, which is God's Word, in order to produce and develop faith. As we feast upon God's Word, our minds become renewed with His Word, and we have a fresh mental and spiritual attitude (Eph. 4:23, 24).

Likewise, we are to present our bodies a living sacrifice, holy, acceptable unto God (Rom. 12:1) and not let that body dominate us but bring it into subjection to the spirit man (1 Cor. 9:27). God's Word is healing and health to all our flesh (Prov. 4:22). Therefore, God's Word affects each part of us—spirit, soul and body. We become vitally united to the Father, to Jesus and to the Holy Spirit—one with Them (John 16:13-15; John 17:21; Col. 2:10).

Purpose to hear, accept and welcome the Word, and it will take root within your spirit and save your soul. Believe the Word, speak the Word and act on the Word—it is a creative force. The Word is a double-edged sword. Often it places a demand on you to change attitudes and behaviors toward the person for whom you are praying.

Be doers of the Word, and not hearers only, deceiving your own selves (James 1:22). Faith without works, or corresponding action, is dead (James 2:17). Don't be mental assenters—those who agree that the Bible is true but never act on it. *Real faith is acting on God's Word now.* We cannot build faith without practicing the Word. We cannot develop an effective prayer life that is anything but empty words unless God's Word actually has a part in our lives. We are to hold fast to our confession of the Word's truthfulness. Our Lord Jesus is the High Priest of our confession (Heb. 3:1), and He is the guarantee of a better agreement—a more excellent and advantageous covenant (Heb. 7:22).

Prayer does not cause faith to work, but faith causes prayer to work. Therefore, any prayer problem is a lack of knowledge or a problem of doubt.

We can spend fruitless hours in prayer if our hearts are not prepared beforehand. Preparation of the

heart, the spirit, comes from meditation in the Father's
Word, meditation on who we are in Christ, what He is
to us and what the Holy Spirit can mean to us as we
become God-inside minded. As God told Joshua, as
we meditate on the Word day and night, and do
according to all that is written, then shall we make
our way prosperous and have good success (Josh. 1:8).
We are to attend to God's Word, submit to His
sayings, keep them in the center of our hearts and put
away contrary talk (Prov. 4:20-24).

The Holy Spirit is a Divine Helper, and He will
direct our prayer and help us pray when we don't know
how. When we use God's Word in prayer, this is not
something we just rush through uttering once, and we
are finished. Do not be mistaken. There is nothing
"magical" or "manipulative" about it—no set pattern or
device in order to satisfy what we want or think out of
our flesh. Instead we are holding God's Word before
Him. Jesus said we should ask the Father in His name.

*We expect His divine intervention while we choose
not to look at the things that are seen but at things that*

are unseen, for the things that are seen are subject to change (2 Cor. 4:18).

Prayer based upon the Word rises above the senses, contacts the Author of the Word and sets His spiritual laws into motion. It is not just saying prayers that gets results, but it is spending time with the Father, learning His wisdom, drawing on His strength, being filled with His quietness and basking in His love that bring results to our prayers. Praise the Lord!

The prayers in this book are designed to teach and train you in the art of prayer. As you pray them, you will be reinforcing the prayer armor which we have been instructed to put on in Ephesians 6:11. The fabric from which the armor is made is the Word of God. We are to live by every word that proceeds from the mouth of God. We desire the whole counsel of God because we know it changes us. By receiving that counsel, you will be **...transformed (changed) by the [entire] renewal of your mind—by its new ideals and attitude—so that you may prove [for yourselves] what is the good and acceptable and perfect will of**

**God, even the thing which is good and acceptable
and perfect [in His sight for you]** (Rom. 12:2 AMP).

The prayers for personal concerns may be used as
intercessory prayers for others by simply praying them
in the third person, changing the pronouns *I* or *we* to
the name(s) of the person(s) for whom you are inter-
ceding, and adjusting the verbs accordingly. The Holy
Spirit is your Helper. Remember that you cannot
control another's will, but your prayers prepare the way
for the individual to hear truth and understand truth.

An often-asked question is "How many times
should I pray the same prayer?"

The answer is simple: You pray until you know
that the answer is fixed in your heart. After that, you
need to repeat the prayer whenever adverse circumstances or long delays cause you to be tempted to
doubt that your prayer has been heard and your
request granted.

The Word of God is your weapon against the
temptation to lose heart and grow weary in your prayer
life. When that Word of promise becomes fixed in
your heart, you will find yourself praising, giving glory

to God for the answer, even when the only evidence you have of that answer is your own faith. Reaffirming your faith enforces the triumph and victory of our Lord Jesus Christ.

Another question frequently asked is this: "When we repeat prayers more than once, aren't we praying 'vain repetitions'?"

Obviously, such people are referring to the admonition of Jesus when He told His disciples: **And when you pray do not (multiply words, repeating the same ones over and over, and) heap up phrases as the Gentiles do, for they think they will be heard for their much speaking** (Matt. 6:7 AMP). Praying the Word of God is not praying the kind of prayer that the "heathen" pray. You will note in 1 Kings 18:25-29 the manner of prayer that was offered to the gods who could not hear. That is not the way you and I pray. The words that we speak are not vain, but they are spirit and life, and mighty through God to the pulling down of strongholds. We have a God Whose eyes are over the righteous and Whose ears are open to us: When we pray, He hears us.

You are the righteousness of God in Christ Jesus, and your prayers will avail much. They will bring salvation to the sinner, deliverance to the oppressed, healing to the sick and prosperity to the poor. They will usher in the next move of God on the earth. In addition to affecting outward circumstances and other people, your prayers will also affect you.

In the very process of praying, your life will be changed as you go from faith to faith and from glory to glory.

As a Christian, your first priority is to love the Lord your God with your entire being, and your neighbor as yourself. You are called to be an intercessor, a man or woman of prayer. You are to seek the face of the Lord as you inquire, listen, meditate and consider in the temple of the Lord.

The will of the Lord for your life is the same as it is for the life of every one of "God's set-apart ones": **...seek ye first the kingdom of God, and his righteousness; and all these things shall be added unto you** (Matt. 6:33).

Personal Confessions

Jesus is Lord over my spirit, my soul and my body (Phil. 2:9-11).

Jesus has been made unto me wisdom, righteousness, sanctification and redemption. I can do all things through Christ, Who strengthens me (1 Cor. 1:30; Phil. 4:13).

The Lord is my shepherd. I do not want. My God supplies all my need according to His riches in glory in Christ Jesus (Ps. 23, Phil. 4:19).

I do not fret or have anxiety about anything. I do not have a care (Phil. 4:6, 1 Peter 5:6, 7).

I am the Body of Christ. I am redeemed from the curse because Jesus bore my sicknesses and carried my diseases in His own body. By His stripes I am healed. I forbid any sickness or disease to operate in my body. Every organ, every tissue of my body, functions in the perfection in which God created it to function. I honor

God and bring glory to Him in my body (Gal. 3:13; Matt. 8:17; 1 Peter 2:24; 1 Cor. 2:16).

I have the mind of Christ and hold the thoughts, feelings and purposes of His heart (1 Cor. 2:16).

I am a believer and not a doubter. I hold fast to my confession of faith. I decide to walk by faith and practice faith. My faith comes by hearing and hearing by the Word of God. Jesus is the author and the developer of my faith (Heb. 4:14, 11:6; Rom. 10:17; Heb. 12:2).

The love of God has been shed abroad in my heart by the Holy Spirit, and His love abides in me richly. I keep myself in the Kingdom of light, in love, in the Word; and the wicked one touches me not (Rom. 5:5; 1 John 4:16, 5:18).

I tread upon serpents and scorpions and over all the power of the enemy. I take my shield of faith and quench his every fiery dart. Greater is He Who is in me than he who is in the world (Ps. 91:13; Eph. 6:16; 1 John 4:4).

I am delivered from this present evil world. I am seated with Christ in heavenly places. I reside in the Kingdom of God's dear Son. The law of the Spirit of life in Christ Jesus has made me free from the law of sin and death (Gal. 1:4; Eph. 2:6; Col. 1:13; Rom. 8:2).

I fear not, for God has given me a spirit of power, of love and of a sound mind. God is on my side (2 Tim. 1:7; Rom. 8:31).

I hear the voice of the Good Shepherd. I hear my Father's voice, and the voice of a stranger I will not follow. I roll my works upon the Lord. I commit and trust them wholly to Him. He will cause my thoughts to become agreeable to His will, and so shall my plans be established and succeed (John 10:27; Prov. 16:3).

I am a world overcomer because I am born of God. I represent the Father and Jesus well. I am a useful member in the Body of Christ. I am His workmanship re-created in Christ Jesus. My Father God is all the while effectually at work in me both to will and do His good pleasure (1 John 5:4,5; Eph. 2:10; Phil. 2:13).

I let the Word dwell in me richly. He Who began a good work in me will continue until the day of Christ (Col. 3:16; Phil. 1:6).

Part 1

Prayers
for Individual
Concerns

Beginning Each Day

Father, as the _____
(owner, president, chairman, manager, supervisor) of
_____ *(name of company)*, I come
before You rejoicing, for this is the day which You have
made and I will be glad in it. To obey is better than
sacrifice, so I am making a decision to submit to Your
will today, that my plans and purposes may be
conducted in a manner that will bring honor and glory
to You. Cause me to be spiritually and mentally alert in
this time of meditation and prayer.

It is into Your keeping that I place my family—my
parents, spouse, children and grandchildren—knowing
that You are able to keep that which I commit to You
against that day. Thank You for the angels that You
have commanded concerning me and my family to
guard us in all our ways; they will lift us up in their
hands so that we will not strike our foot against a stone.

Thank You, Lord, for the tremendous success that my associates and I have experienced in our organization and for the increase in profits and productivity we have enjoyed. Thank You for Your faithfulness to us day by day and for helping us to become all that You desire us to be.

Thank You, Father, for helping to make us a company that continues to grow and expand. We recognize that without Your help, it would not be possible. Without Your direction and guidance, we would be failures; with it we can prosper and have good success. I continue to thank You for the many blessings that You have poured out upon us all.

I especially thank You for the co-laborers with whom I will be interacting today. Give me words of wisdom, words of grace, that I might encourage them and build them up.

Father, I kneel before You, from Whom Your whole family in heaven and on earth derives its name. I pray that out of Your glorious riches You may strengthen each one with power through Your Spirit in the inner being, so that Christ may dwell in each heart through faith.

Now to Him Who is able to do immeasurably more than all we ask or imagine, according to His power that is at work within us, to Him be the glory in this company and in Christ Jesus throughout all generations, for ever and ever! In Jesus' name I pray. Amen.

Scripture References

Psalm 118:24   Lamentations 3:22,23
1 Samuel 15:22   Joshua 1:8
2 Timothy 1:12   Ephesians 3:14-17 NIV
Psalm 91:11,12 NIV   Ephesians 3:20 NIV

Knowing God's Will

Father, I thank You that You are instructing me and teaching me in the way I should go and that You are guiding me with Your eye. I thank You for Your guidance and leadership concerning Your will, Your plan and Your purpose for my life. I do hear the voice of the Good Shepherd, for I know You and follow You. You lead me in the paths of righteousness for Your name's sake.

In the name of Jesus, I refuse to be conformed to this world (this age), [fashioned after and adapted to its external, superficial customs], but I submit to the transformation by the [entire] renewal of my mind [by its new ideals and its new attitude], so that I may prove [for myself] what is Your good and acceptable and perfect will, even the thing which is good and acceptable and perfect [in Your sight for me].

Thank You, Father, that my path is growing brighter and brighter until it reaches the full light of day. As I follow You, Lord, I believe my path is becoming clearer each day.

Thank You, Father, that Jesus was made unto me wisdom. Confusion is not a part of my life. I am not confused about Your will for me. I trust in You and lean not unto my own understanding. As I acknowledge You in all my ways, You direct my paths. I believe that as I trust in You completely, You will show me the path of life.

Thank You, Father, in Jesus' name. Amen.

Scripture References

Psalm 32:8	Proverbs 4:18
John 10:3,4	1 Corinthians 1:30
Psalm 23:3	Proverbs 3:5,6
Romans 12:2 AMP	Psalm 16:11

Being Equipped for Success

Father, I thank You that the entrance of Your words gives light. I thank You that Your Word which You speak (and which I speak) is alive and full of power [making it active, operative, energizing and effective].

I thank You, Father, that [You have given me a spirit] of power and of love and of a calm and well-balanced mind and discipline and self-control. I have Your power and ability and sufficiency, for You have qualified me [making me to be fit and worthy and sufficient] as a minister and dispenser of a new covenant [of salvation through Christ].

In the name of Jesus, I walk out of the realm of failure into the arena of success, giving thanks to You, Father, for You have qualified me and made me fit to share the portion which is the inheritance of the saints (Your holy people) in the light.

Father, You have delivered and drawn me to Your-self out of the control and the dominion of darkness (failure, doubt and fear) and have transferred me into the Kingdom of the Son of Your love.

I praise God, the Father of my Lord Jesus Christ, Who has blessed me with every blessing in heaven, because I belong to Christ. Your divine power has given me everything I need for life and godliness through my knowledge of Him Who called me by His own glory and goodness. I rejoice in Jesus Who has come that I might have life and have it more abundantly.

I am a new creation, for I am (engrafted) in Christ, the Messiah. The old [previous moral and spiritual condition] has passed away. Behold, the fresh and new has come! I forget those things which are behind me and reach forth unto those things which are before me. I am crucified with Christ: Nevertheless I live; yet not I, but Christ lives in me; and the life which I now live in the flesh I live by the faith of the Son of God, Who loved me and gave Himself for me.

Father, I attend to Your Word. I consent and submit to Your sayings. Your words shall not depart from my sight; I will keep them in the center of my heart. For they are life (success) to me, healing and health to all my flesh. I keep and guard my heart with all vigilance; and above all, that I guard, for out of it flow the springs of life.

I will not let mercy and kindness and truth forsake me. I bind them about my neck; I write them upon the tablet of my heart. So therefore I will find favor, good understanding and high esteem in the sight [or judgment] of God and man.

Father, my delight and desire are in Your law, and on it I habitually meditate (ponder and study—by day and by night. Therefore I am like a tree firmly planted [and tended] by the streams of water, ready to bring forth my fruit in my season; my leaf also shall not fade or wither, and everything I do shall prosper [and come to maturity].

Now thanks be to You, Father, Who always cause me to triumph in Christ!

In Jesus' name I pray, amen.

Scripture References

Psalm 119:130

Hebrews 4:12 AMP

2 Timothy 1:7 AMP

2 Corinthians 3:5 AMP

Colossians 1:12,13 AMP

Ephesians 1:3 TLB

2 Peter 1:3 NIV

John 10:10 AMP

2 Corinthians 5:17 AMP

Philippians 3:13

Galatians 2:20

Proverbs 4:20-23 AMP

Proverbs 3:3,4 AMP

Psalm 1:2,3 AMP

2 Corinthians 2:14

Setting Proper Priorities

Father, too often I allow urgency to dictate my schedule, and I am asking You to help me establish priorities in my work. I confess my weakness* of procrastination and lack of organization. My desire is to live purposefully and worthily and accurately as a wise, sensible, intelligent person.

You have given me a seven-day week—six days to work and the seventh day to rest. I desire to make the most of the time [buying up each opportunity]. Help me plan my day, and stay focused on my assignments.

In the name of Jesus, I demolish and smash warped philosophies concerning time management, tear down barriers erected against the truth of God, and fit every loose thought, emotion and impulse into the structure of life shaped by Christ. I clear my mind of every obstruction and build a life of obedience into maturity.

*If you do not know your strengths and weaknesses, ask the Holy Spirit to reveal them to you. The Lord speaks to us: "My grace is sufficient for you, for power is perfected in weakness" (2 Cor. 12:9 NAS).

Father, You are in charge of my work and my plans. I plan the way I want to live, but You alone make me able to live it. Help me to organize my efforts, schedule my activities and budget my time.

Jesus, You want me to relax. It pleases You when I am not preoccupied with getting, so I can respond to God's giving. I know You, Father God, and how You work. I steep my life in God-reality, God-initiative and God-provisions.

By the grace given me, I will not worry about missing out, and my everyday human concerns will be met. I purpose in my heart to seek (aim at and strive after) first of all Your Kingdom, Lord, and Your righteousness [Your way of doing and being right], and then all these things taken together will be given me besides.

Father, Your Word is my compass, and it helps me see my life as complete in Christ. I cast all my cares, worries and concerns over on You, that I might be well-balanced (temperate, sober of mind), vigilant and cautious at all times.

I tune my ears to the word of wisdom and set my heart on a life of understanding. I make insight my priority.

Father, You sent Jesus that I might have life and have it more abundantly. Help me remember that my relationships with You and with others are more important than anything else. Amen.

Scripture References

Ephesians 5:15-16 AMP

2 Corinthians 10:5-6 MESSAGE

Matthew 11:29 MESSAGE, AMP

1 Peter 5:7-8 AMP

John 10:10

Genesis 2:2 NIV

Proverbs 16:3, 9 MESSAGE

Colossians 2:10

Proverbs 2:3 MESSAGE

Assuring the Success of a Business

Father, I come before You with thanksgiving. You have qualified me and made me fit to share the portion which is the inheritance of the saints (Your holy people) in the light. You have delivered me out of the power of darkness and translated me into the Kingdom of Your dear Son.

As I know You better, You will give me, through Your great power, everything I need for living a truly good life. You even share Your own glory and Your own goodness with me! And by that same mighty power You have given me all the other rich and wonderful blessings You promised; for instance, the promise to save me from the lust and rottenness all around me, and to give me Your own character.

You have delivered me out of the power of darkness and translated me into the Kingdom of Your dear Son.

Where Your Word is, there is light and understanding. Your Word does not return to You void, but it always accomplishes what it is sent to do.

I am a joint-heir with Jesus, and as Your son/daughter, I accept that the communication of my faith is effectual by the acknowledging of every good thing which is in me in Christ Jesus.

Father, I commit my works (the plans and cares of my business) to You, trusting them wholly to You. Since You are effectually at work in me [You cause my thoughts to become agreeable with Your will] so that my (business) plans shall be established and succeed.

In the name of Jesus, I submit to every kind of wisdom and understanding (practical insight and prudence) which You have lavished upon me in accordance with the riches and generosity of Your gracious favor.

Father, I affirm that I obey Your Word by making an honest living with my own hands so that I may be able to give to those in need. In Your strength and according to Your grace I provide for myself and my own family.

Thank You, Father, for making all grace (every favor and earthly blessing) come to me in abundance, so that I, having all sufficiency in all things, may abound to every good work.

Father, thank You for the ministering spirits that You have assigned to go forth to minister on my behalf and bring in trade. Jesus said that those who put their faith and trust in Him are the light of the world. In His name my light shall so shine before all men that they may see my good works and glorify You, my heavenly Father.

Thank You for the grace to remain diligent in seeking knowledge and skill in areas in which I am inexperienced. I ask You for wisdom and the ability to understand righteousness, justice and fair dealing [in every area and relationship]. I affirm that I am faithful and committed to Your Word. My life and business are founded upon its principles.

Thank You, Father, for the success of my business!

In Jesus' name I pray, amen.

Scripture References

Colossians 1:12 AMP

Colossians 1:13

2 Peter 1:3-5 TLB

Psalm 119:130

Isaiah 55:11

2 Corinthians 6:16,18

Philemon 6

Proverbs 16:3 AMP

Philippians 2:13 AMP

Ephesians 1:7,8 AMP

Ephesians 4:28 AMP

1 Timothy 5:8 AMP

2 Corinthians 9:8 AMP

2 Corinthians 9:8

Hebrews 1:14

Matthew 5:14,16

Proverbs 22:29 AMP

Proverbs 2:9 AMP

Proverbs 4:20-22 AMP

Enjoying Prosperity

Father, in the name of Your Son, Jesus, I confess Your Word over my finances this day. As I do so, I say it with my mouth and believe it in my heart and know that Your Word will not return to You void, but will accomplish what You send it to do.

Therefore, I believe in the name of Jesus that all my needs are met, according to Philippians 4:19. I believe that because I have given tithes and offerings to further Your cause, Father, gifts will be given to me; good measure, pressed down, shaken together and running over will they be poured into my bosom. For with the measure I deal out, it will be measured back to me.

Father, You have delivered me out of the power of darkness into the Kingdom of Your dear Son, where I have taken my place as Your child. I thank You that You have assumed Your place as my Father and have made Your home with me. You are taking care of me and even now are enabling me to walk in love, in wisdom and in the fullness of fellowship with Your Son.

Father, I thank You that Your ministering spirits are now free to minister for me and bring in the necessary finances.

I confess that You are a very present help in trouble, and that You are more than enough. You are able to make all grace (every favor and earthly blessing) come to me in abundance, so that I am always and under all circumstances [furnished in abundance for every good work and charitable donation].

Thank You, Lord, in Jesus' name. Amen.

Scripture References

Isaiah 55:11

Philippians 4:19

Mark 10:29,30

Luke 6:38

Colossians 1:13

2 Corinthians 6:16,18

Matthew 18:18

Hebrews 1:14

Psalm 46:1

2 Corinthians 9:8 AMP

NOTE TO THE READER

The above prayer releases the light of God's Word into the earth and prepares you to stand against all the strategies of the enemy. You are strong in the Lord and in the power of His might; clothed in the armor of God and with the Holy Spirit as your Helper, you are ready to enforce the triumphant victory Jesus won at Calvary.

Submit to the will of God, and resist Satan. When Satan tempts you to worry, fret and doubt, you have weapons of warfare that are mighty unto God to the pulling down of strongholds. Praise God with the voice of triumph, and withstand the enemy by declaring, "It is written..." just as Jesus did in the fourth chapter of Luke.

One weapon of spiritual warfare is God's Word in your mouth. Another is praise. Turn your attention to heavenly things—keep your mind focused on the answer with great expectation. Take your thoughts captive and bring them into obedience to the Word. Don't give undue attention to the devil. The following is an example of how you enforce the victory Jesus won for you when He defeated Satan and made a public display of his defeat (Col. 2:15).

PRAYER

Father, I thank You for the finished work at Calvary. Jesus said that the gates of hell shall not prevail against the church, and I am a member of Your Body, the church, clothed in the armor of God. The counsel of Satan cannot stand, because Jesus is my Lord.

Speak to your doubts: It is written and I believe that my God will supply all that I need from His glorious resources in Christ Jesus.

Displace your fears: It is written that my God gives me seed for sowing, and I give tithes and offerings, bringing them to the storehouse. He rebukes the destroyer for my sake, and I am blessed in the market-place.

Speak to worry: Great is the Lord, Who delights in the welfare of His servant! My tongue shall tell of His righteousness and of His praise all the day long.

My emotions shall no longer control my spending habits. I choose to be well-balanced, and in the name of Jesus I bind my emotions to the control of the Holy Spirit. I resist the devil, and crush the stronghold of denial. Truth enables me to speak truly, deal truly and live truly in all the affairs of life. I seek out and submit to godly counsel, and I receive knowledge, wisdom and understanding for managing my finances.

Oh, my God, you have seen me, and You are not silent! You are not far from me! You have awakened for my right, for my cause! Let those who would defraud, steal or cheat me be put to shame and confusion altogether. I bind the strong man and command him to bring back everything he has stolen from me.

Father, You have delivered me from the authority of darkness and translated me into the Kingdom of Your dear Son. Now I am blessed with all spiritual blessings in heavenly places in Christ Jesus, my Lord. I seek first the Kingdom of God and His righteousness, and all things are added unto me.

On the authority of Your Word, I declare the Lordship of Jesus Christ over my finances, my giving, my spending, my savings and my investments!

All glory be to my God and my Father for ever and ever, amen!

Scripture References

Matthew 16:18

Ephesians 6

Philippians 4:19 PHILLIPS

2 Corinthians 9:10

Malachi 3:10,11

1 Peter 5:8

James 4:7

2 Corinthians 10:3-6

Ephesians 4:17 AMP

Psalm 35:22-28 RSV

Colossians 1:13

Ephesians 1:3

Matthew 6:33

Finding Favor With Others

Father, You make Your face to shine upon me and enlighten me, and You are gracious (kind, merciful and giving favor) to me. I am the head and not the tail, above only and not beneath.

Thank You for bestowing Your favor upon me because I seek Your Kingdom and Your righteousness and diligently seek good. I am a blessing to You, Lord, and a blessing to _____ *(name them: family, neighbors, business associates, etc.)*. Grace (favor) is with me because I love the Lord Jesus in sincerity.

You extend favor, honor and love to me, and I flow in Your love, Father. You are pouring out upon me the spirit of favor. You crown me with glory and honor, for I am Your child—Your workmanship.

I am a success because I am very special to You, Lord. I am growing in You—waxing strong in spirit.

Father, You give me knowledge and skill in all learning and wisdom. You bring me to find favor,

compassion and loving-kindness with _____
(names). I obtain favor in the sight of all who look
upon me, in the name of Jesus.

I am filled with Your fullness—rooted and
grounded in love. You are doing exceeding abundantly
above all that I ask or think, for Your mighty power is
taking over in my life.

Thank You, Father, that I am increasing in favor
with You and with man.

In Jesus' name I pray, amen.

Scripture References

Numbers 6:25 AMP	Ephesians 2:10 AMP
Deuteronomy 28:13	Luke 2:40
Matthew 6:33	Daniel 1:17
Proverbs 11:27	Daniel 1:9 AMP
Ephesians 6:24	Esther 2:15 AMP
Zechariah 12:10 AMP	Ephesians 3:19,17,20
Psalm 8:5 AMP	Luke 2:52

Being Protected While Traveling

Father, I confess Your Word over my travel plans
and know that Your Word does not return to You void,
but it accomplishes what You send it to do. I give You
thanks for moving quickly to perform Your Word and
fulfill its promises.

As I prepare to travel, I rejoice in the promises
that Your Word holds for protection and safety of
the righteous. Only You, Father, make me live in
safety. I trust in You and dwell in Your protection.
If I should face any problems or trouble, I will run
to You, Lord, my strong tower and shelter in times
of need. Believing in Your written Word, I speak
peace, safety and success over my travel plans, in
Jesus' name.

Because I am Your child, my path of travel is
preserved, and angels keep charge over me and
surround my means of transportation. I will proceed
with my travel plans without fear of accidents, prob-

lems or any type of frustrations. I have Your peace within and will allow fear no place as I travel. You, Lord, deliver me from every type of evil and preserve me for Your Kingdom. I stand confident that my travel plans will not be disrupted or confused.

Thank You, Father, that in every situation I encounter You are there to protect me. No matter by what type of transportation I choose to travel, You have redeemed me and will protect me. The earth and all things on it are under Your command. You are my heavenly Father, and I am Your child. Through my faith in You, I have the power to tread on serpents and have power over all the enemy. No food or drink will harm me while I am away from home. No matter where I may go, I am protected.

Father, I give You the glory in this situation. Thank You that as I keep Your ways before me, I will be secure. Your mercy is upon me, and my travel will be safe. Not a hair on my head will perish.

Thank You, Father, for upholding me with Your right hand of righteousness. You are worthy, my Lord and God, to receive glory and honor and power, for You created all things, and by Your will they were created and have their being.

In Jesus' name I pray, amen.

Scripture References

Isaiah 55:11	Philippians 4:7
Jeremiah 1:12	2 Timothy 1:7
Psalm 4:8	Isaiah 43:1-3
Psalm 91:1	Hosea 2:18
Proverbs 18:10	Luke 10:19
Proverbs 29:25	Psalm 91:13
Mark 11:23,24	Luke 21:18
Proverbs 2:8	Mark 16:18
Psalm 91:11,12	Isaiah 41:10
2 Timothy 4:18	Revelation 4:11 NIV

Part II

Special
Prayers
for Employers

Conducting a Meeting

Father, in the name of Jesus, may Your wisdom prevail today in our meeting. Help each of us to be quick to listen, slow to speak and slow to become angry, for man's anger does not bring about the righteous life that You desire.

Lord, I recognize Your Holy Spirit and welcome Him to the meeting, acknowledging our dependence upon His presence and guidance. With His help, I purpose to respect and regard every individual's opinions as valuable and worthy of consideration. Knowing that a soft answer turns away wrath, I will be polite and courteous in all our deliberations.

Help each one of us to offer opinions at the appropriate times and to resist any feelings of self-pity or self-aggrandizement. Guard us from thinking that our opinions are not being heard.

I pray for those who have to deal with rejection. Help them to know that any negation of their opinions or suggestions is not personal.

Should my own opinions be rejected, I refuse to believe that I, personally, am rejected. I will remember that my opinions are not me.

Father, Your love in me does not insist on its own rights or its own way, for it is not self-seeking. I submit to the wisdom that comes from heaven, for it is pure, peace-loving, considerate, full of mercy and good fruit, impartial and sincere. As a peacemaker, I sow in peace, reaping a harvest of righteousness.

Thank You, Father, for wisdom that is from above.

In Jesus' name I pray, amen.

Scripture References

Ephesians 1:17	1 Peter 5:5 NIV
James 1:19,20 NIV	Romans 12:10 NIV
John 16:13	1 Corinthians 13:5 AMP
Proverbs 15:1	James 3:17,18 NIV

PRAYER FOR CONVENING A MEETING

Father, we all come into agreement concerning this meeting today. Thank You that it will be productive. Help us to stay on track and keep focused on the agenda. Bring to our minds solutions to the problems that we are facing. Help each one of us present to be able to make a contribution of value and worth to the process of this meeting.

Thank You for the liberty to discuss openly and freely without strife or anger. Help us to speak our minds without fear of ridicule or sarcasm.

Thank You that we all have understanding hearts toward one another and toward any item that we discuss today.

Help us to consider all the facts and come to a definitive plan of action concerning the direction that we need to take. Help us not to overanalyze or to be hasty and move too quickly, but rather to respond effectively and efficiently to any problem that needs our attention. Help us to operate and flow together as a team.

In Jesus' name we pray, amen.

Scripture References

Matthew 18:19 AMP

2 Corinthians 3:17 AMP

Proverbs 5:18

James 3:16 AMP

James 1:19,20 NIV

Ephesians 4:31,32 NIV

Colossians 3:8 NIV

Philippians 2:3 NIV

Proverbs 1:5 AMP

Proverbs 2:2 AMP

Proverbs 21:3 NIV

Proverbs 29:20 AMP

Psalm 133:1

PRAYER FOR ENDING A MEETING

Father, we thank You for this meeting.

We believe that we have accomplished what we set out to do. Now we thank You that we take away from this meeting the facts and data we need to act decisively and to perform to the best of our ability any assignments that have been made.

Thank You, Father, that everyone has something to do and that each one does it effectively and efficiently. Thank You that we have all the information we need to make right decisions.

Thank You, Father, for a fruitful and productive time together.

In Jesus' name we pray, amen.

Scripture References

Colossians 4:17 AMP   James 1:5 AMP
Proverbs 21:2 NIV   John 15:1,2 NIV

Making a Difficult Decision

Father, I bring this decision before You. It is a difficult one for me to make in the natural, but I know that with You it can be an easy one.

I ask You, Lord, to help me see both sides of this issue and to consider all the facts involved in it. Help me to properly evaluate both the positive and negative attributes of this situation.

Lord, I recognize that an important part of being an excellent manager is decisiveness. In processing the information and considering the possible repercussions or benefits of this decision, help me to avoid the paralysis of analysis. Help me to get the information I need and to evaluate it carefully and wisely.

Help me, Father, to hear Your voice, and so to make the right and correct decision in this case. Keep me from acting in haste but also from delaying too long to reach a decision.

Father, help me not to be influenced by my own personal wants or desires concerning this matter under consideration. Instead, help me to perceive and choose what is best for my department or company, regardless of how I may feel about it personally. Help me to undertake and carry out this decision-making process accurately and objectively.

Thank You for Your guidance and direction in this situation.

In Jesus' name I pray, amen.

Scripture References

Isaiah 11:2 AMP   John 10:27

Colossians 4:1 NIV   Philippians 2:3 NIV

Proverbs 28:1   Judges 6:12

Preparing a Budget

Lord, I ask for Your help concerning the budget that I must prepare. I recognize, Father, that it is necessary for the proper operation of my department and/or company. I know that it can be a tedious and time-consuming job, so I ask You to help me not to overlook anything that needs to be included or considered.

Using the knowledge that I have, and depending on the leading of the Holy Spirit, I ask You to help me to accurately estimate expenses and income. Show me what I cannot see so I can properly assess our current and future situations. Help me to anticipate unforeseen events so I can determine what our future needs will be and make provision now to meet them.

Lord, help me to view this budget as a management tool, to see it not just as a form to be completed in order to appease the accounting department, but as an accurate presentation of the present and future financial situation of my department and/or company.

Help me to be conservative in my estimation of projected income and judicious in my estimation of projected expenses. Help me to arrive at the most accurate figures possible in the preparation of this vital document.

Thank You for Your guidance, direction and wisdom.

In Jesus' name I pray, amen.

Scripture References

Deuteronomy 8:18	John 16:13
Isaiah 48:17 NIV	Luke 12:2 NIV
Deuteronomy 28:8,11-13 NIV	James 1:5

Analyzing a Report

Lord, I come to You in prayer before I begin to analyze this report before me. I recognize that this is information I need in order to function properly and to fulfill my responsibilities.

I ask You, Father, to help me to analyze this report accurately and to draw from it what I need to make wise decisions.

Show me, Lord, not only those things that are obvious, but also those that are not readily apparent to the natural human eye. Increase my understanding. If there is more information needed, help me to determine what it is and how to go about getting it.

Help me to be able to assimilate vital data and facts and to reduce them to their bare essentials. Give me discernment to notice any trends, either positive or negative, that are developing within my department and/or company. Help me to take the information and knowledge I gain and use it to better carry out my duties.

Help me to take what You are showing me and apply it to my daily activities so that I may enhance my overall job performance and improve the success rate of my department and this organization.

In Jesus' name I pray, amen.

Scripture References

Matthew 7:7,8 NIV   Proverbs 2:11 NIV

Ephesians 1:17   Daniel 11:32 AMP

Ephesians 3:20 AMP   Joshua 1:8 NIV

Proverbs 4:11 AMP   Matthew 6:33

Creating New Products and/or Services

Lord, You have said that You will give us new and creative ideas, that the Holy Spirit will show us things to come. I request that You send Your Holy Spirit now to help us in the creating and developing of new products and services.

Father, You know what the market needs are now and what they will be in the future. You know what products and services will be a blessing to people's lives. Give us new ideas and innovative concepts so that we may develop newer and better goods and services for our company.

Give us ideas, Lord, that translate into products and services, which translate into successful growth and blessings to us and others.

In Jesus' name I pray, amen.

Scripture References

Proverbs 8:12

Proverbs 18:21

Daniel 10:12

John 16:13

Proverbs 17:27 AMP

Daniel 5:14 AMP

Daniel 6:3 AMP

Philippians 1:10 AMP

Undertaking a New Project

Lord, I lift up to You this new project which we are considering. I feel that it is one we should be a part of, something we should do, but I seek Your wisdom concerning it.

If it is not of You, Lord, please put a check in our spirits. Direct us to stop planning and working on it and to put a halt to any further waste of time and energy.

If it is of You, Father, then I thank You for Your counsel and assistance concerning it. Give us understanding and discernment in the preparation stages as we gather the information we need to devise a course of action and to plan the budget. Help us to accumulate the facts and figures we need to carry out this plan in accordance with Your will and purpose.

Thank You, Lord, for Your insight and wisdom. I ask You to give each of us guidance and direction by Your Holy Spirit so we will know how to assimilate the information we gather and use it to maximum advantage. Reveal to us any hidden costs or expenses so that we can take them into account in preparing an accurate budget and detailed forecast of both time and money.

Give all of us involved in this project the ability to concentrate our attention and focus our efforts so that we can successfully complete this undertaking and thereby bring honor and glory to You.

In Jesus' name I pray, amen.

Scripture References

Proverbs 8:12 AMP   Ephesians 1:8,9,17 AMP

Isaiah 11:2 NIV   Luke 12:2 NIV

Jeremiah 29:11-13   Romans 12:2 NIV

Jeremiah 33:3 NIV

Purchasing New Equipment

Lord, I come to You concerning this new piece of equipment that we are considering.

Lord, according to all the sources of information available to us, I have determined that we do need this particular item. If we do not really need it, or if there is another way we can achieve the same results without buying it outright, please speak to my heart and tell me. If we do need to buy it, then I ask You to give us favor as we consult with potential sellers and compare prices and terms.

Father, give us wisdom in this venture. First of all, help us to accurately identify the benefits and services that this piece of equipment will provide for us so that we can buy with confidence that it will fulfill our needs.

Help us, Lord, to determine the true value and worth of our purchase. Help us not to make the mistake of buying either the cheapest or the most expensive product simply because of its price. Instead, help us to choose the one that will provide maximum quality at the most economical cost. Help us to balance long-term return with short-term outlay.

Help us to determine exactly how this piece of equipment will contribute to our efforts and increase our output and quality of production. Show us ways that it can help us to save money by reducing expenses.

Help us to make the best sales and service contract possible. Help us to identify the maintenance that will be necessary to keep this equipment running at maximum efficiency.

Give us discernment as we consider different dealers and examine their claims, track records and professional references. Give us wisdom so that we can hear and understand what is being said to us and be sensitive to what is not being said.

In all our deliberations, help us, Lord, to establish whether this is the right piece of equipment for our needs and to get the very best value for the money we spend.

In Jesus' name I pray, amen.

Scripture References

1 Corinthians 4:5 NIV	Psalm 5:12
2 Corinthians 4:2 NIV	1 John 5:14,15
1 Corinthians 4:2 AMP	Revelation 3:7,8 AMP

Choosing a New Bank

Lord, I pray concerning the choice of a new bank. In order to carry on the operations of our business, we must locate a sound financial institution that can and will properly handle our money matters.

I ask You, Lord, to help us find such a bank: one that will be sensitive to our needs, that will believe in us as an organization and that will be concerned about us as individuals—not just as another account number.

Father, we are looking for people with whom we can develop a long-term relationship and grow with as the needs of our company grow. It is our desire to be a blessing to them just as they bless us.

Help us, Lord, to look into the future and make wise decisions, choices that will be best for the company and everyone in it—not only now, but in the years to come.

Thank You, Father, for leading us to the right bank and for giving us favor with its officers and them with us. Thank You for bringing us together so that we might establish an agreement—a partnership—that is right for them and for us, one that is profitable for their operation as well as ours.

In Jesus' name I pray, amen.

Scripture References

Proverbs 8:14 NIV

Ephesians 6:7,8 NIV

Jeremiah 33:3 TLB

Proverbs 19:21 NIV

Psalm 5:12

Proverbs 8:32-35 NIV

Proverbs 16:2,3 NIV

Increasing Sales

Father, I pray concerning the sales of our company.

I lift up to Your throne of grace everyone who is involved in selling, whether by phone, in person or through the mail. I ask that You continue to bless them and their efforts on behalf of our organization.

Thank You, Father, for Your wisdom and Your favor upon us as, through our sales force, we share the benefits of our goods/services. Thank You that You give our people favor with our customers as they talk to them.

Father, I ask that You help our salespeople to know what the needs of our customers are. Help them never to oversell, but always to adequately, effectively and efficiently present our products/services.

Give us wisdom and insight in the development of our sales promotions and techniques. Help us always to be honest and upfront. Help us always to explain the benefits of our products/services in a clear and accurate way.

I ask You, Father, that You guide our salespeople so that they are able to respond quickly to any objection to the purchase or our products/services. Give them favor when setting up appointments and making sales presentations. Help them to offer the products/services in the proper way.

Thank You, Father, that there is a need for our products/services, and that You continue to open new doors and provide new markets for them. Thank You that we have growth with our existing customers on a regular basis. Thank You that we are increasing sales and adding new markets daily. To You we give all honor and glory for our success.

In Jesus' name I pray, amen.

Scripture References

Deuteronomy 28:6,8,13 NIV   Hebrews 13:18 AMP

Psalm 1:1-3 NIV   Psalm 119:165 AMP

Psalm 5:12   Revelation 3:7,8 NIV

Proverbs 8:12   Matthew 7:7,8 NIV

Romans 12:17 NIV

Handling Accounts Payable

Father, I pray concerning our accounts payable.

I thank You, Lord, first of all, for giving us wisdom in what we buy and how we buy it.

Thank You, Father, that we are budget-driven, that we are sensitive to the even flow of cash through this organization. Thank You that we do not purchase anything we do not need or cannot pay for.

Thank You that You guide us in all our decisions regarding purchases, that You cause us to ask ourselves questions such as "Is this something that we have to have? Is it something that the organization needs to be successful? If so, is this the time to make this purchase?"

Thank You, Lord, that we are able to make all purchases with full confidence that we are doing the right things and that we will have the funds necessary to pay for them in accordance with our purchase agreement.

Thank You that every bill we owe is paid on time, and that we have a good credit rating and a reputation for honesty and integrity with our creditors.

In Jesus' name I pray, amen.

Scripture References

Proverbs 2:6-11 NIV   Isaiah 48:17 AMP

Proverbs 3:32 AMP   Psalm 25:21 TLB

Psalm 37:23 AMP

Handling Accounts Receivable

Father, I lift up those people who are in debt to this organization. I thank You that everyone who owes our company money pays it to us.

For those who are unable to pay because they lack the necessary funds, I thank You for increasing their business and providing them the income needed to meet their financial obligations.

For those, Lord, who order products/services and cannot pay for them because of a lack of foresight or improper budgeting, I ask that You give them wisdom concerning the future. I pray that the eyes of their understanding will be opened and that they will learn to be more diligent in their business dealings.

Lord, concerning those people who fraudulently order products/services with no intention to pay, I ask that You will cause them to see their need to deal justly in all their business transactions. Send the Holy Spirit to convict their hearts and reprove their minds, that they might repent, make things right and follow Your rules and principles.

I pray, Father, for our credit manager. I ask that You give him/her success and favor when gathering information and contacting our debtors, and wisdom and knowledge in making decisions about handling the accounts—especially those that are overdue.

In Jesus' name I pray, amen.

Scripture References

Luke 7:41-43

Deuteronomy 28:12 TLB

Psalm 115:14

Ephesians 1:17,18

Psalm 37:21 NIV

Proverbs 22:29 AMP

John 16:8 NIV

Psalm 5:12

Handling Unpaid Bills

Lord, I come to You concerning these bills that are currently due. As You are aware, we are unable to pay them at this time.

Lord, I know it is right to keep our vendors and debtors informed, and I commit to do so.

I ask You for favor with all those we owe. Give me wisdom as I speak to them concerning the fulfillment of our obligations. Help them to realize, Father, that our inability to pay is not due to fraudulence in our dealings. Assure them that when we incurred these debts, we were operating in full confidence that we would be able to meet the obligations at the time specified. Now that we are unable to do so, I ask You, Father, that You give us favor with them so that we can work out an agreeable plan for retiring these obligations.

I thank You for bringing in the needed funds through increased sales and/or decreased expenses so that we can pay off our outstanding debts as soon as possible.

Thank You, Lord, for all Your help.

In Jesus' name I pray, amen.

Scripture References

Philippians 4:19	Psalm 25:21 AMP
Proverbs 10:4 NIV	Proverbs 10:22 NIV
Psalm 5:12	Proverbs 8:21

Facing a Financial Crisis

Lord, I come to You in this time of great need in the life of our organization. Whatever the cause, we find ourselves in extreme financial need.

First of all, Father, I come against the spirit of fear, in the name of Jesus. I refuse to operate in fear, anxiety or worry concerning this situation. I know it is serious, and I do not approach it flippantly. But I know that if there is fear, anxiety or worry in my heart, it will cloud my judgment and appraisal of the situation. It will make it seem even worse than it really is. It will also block my ability to hear from You.

Father, I give this whole situation to You and ask for Your guidance and direction in rectifying it. If it came about because of any bad decisions I made or any wrong thoughts or actions I engaged in, I repent to You right now. I ask You for forgiveness. Help me to see my mistakes and faults and to do all in my power to overcome and correct them.

Lord, if this financial crisis is the result of my negligence or my irresponsible spending, I ask You to forgive me. Help me to be sensitive to Your voice so that I may hear from You as I seek Your counsel. I open my heart to You. Show me what to do so that such a crisis as this one never occurs again.

Concerning the current need, I ask You to help me and to give me favor with those to whom we owe money. I thank You for an increase in sales so that our income can grow, knowledge so we will know where to cut expenses, and insight so we will know how to budget the money that we do have.

Thank You for supernatural wisdom so we can see how to walk out of this terrible situation. Help us to formulate a plan of recovery, a plan to get from where we are today to where we want to be tomorrow. Help me to communicate that plan clearly and effectively to the ones who will be involved in it.

Lord, send me counselors, those who can help me with this task. Send me people with wisdom and insight concerning this situation, that they might help me perceive and discern Your perfect plan for recovery.

Father, I give myself entirely to You. Thank You that I hear Your voice accurately and distinctly as You reveal to me what to do and how to do it. I ask You to help me identify the reason why we got into this crisis in the first place and to erect safeguards so that it will never happen again.

Thank You for Your forgiveness, Your help, Your wisdom and Your instruction. Thank You that we are totally and completely out of this crisis. I receive it by faith and thank You that it is done, in Jesus' name. Amen.

Scripture References

2 Timothy 1:7

Philippians 4:6 AMP

Ephesians 5:17

John 10:27 NIV

Psalm 5:12

Psalm 115:14

Daniel 2:21-23 AMP

Acts 6:10

Psalm 1:1

Psalm 16:7 AMP

Psalm 73:24

Proverbs 15:22 NIV

Job 22:28

Taking on a New Partner

Father, I feel in my heart that it is important that we take on a new partner in our business. And yet, I know that Your Word is very clear and specific regarding relationships and partnerships. Therefore, I pray, first of all, for Your wisdom, Your instruction. Although I feel in my heart that this move is necessary, if it is not best for the organization, please show us now.

If it is the right thing to do, I ask, Lord, that You send just the right partner, someone who has the same heart and commitment that we have. Above all, we are seeking someone who is committed to You, committed to Your Word and committed to operating and functioning with integrity and honesty. Thank You for a partner who is sincere and above reproach, someone who has the same goals and visions and desires that we do, and yet who brings a different and healthy perspective to the organization.

Lord, once the decision is made and we feel Your peace in our hearts, help us as we examine and select that partner who is to be added to our organization. I pray that he/she will not be someone who will simply duplicate what already exists in the company, but someone with innovative wisdom and insight, a new and fresh approach that will enhance the company's ability to grow and turn a profit.

I pray that You will establish a true and lasting partnership between us, one that is godly in all its ways. I ask for a partnership that will bring this organization to greater heights and at the same time continue to be based on the rock-solid principles and foundations of Your eternal Word.

In Jesus' name I pray, amen.

Scripture References

Proverbs 1:2 AMP

Proverbs 9:9 AMP

Romans 12:16 AMP

Daniel 5:12

Romans 12:16

1 Corinthians 1:10 NIV

Psalm 25:21

Psalm 119:22

Habakkuk 2:2

Colossians 3:15-17

Proverbs 8:10-12 AMP

1 Timothy 4:8 NIV

Lifting Up Employees

Father, I pray for every employee of this organization. I ask that You give me wisdom in my interaction with them. Help me to recognize and develop their individual strengths. Help me to provide them with the necessary tools and resources to get their jobs done. Make me sensitive to their needs, both personal and professional.

Help me to manage what is the most important asset of this organization—that is, its people. When I look at them, help me to see them with my heart as well as my eyes. Give me the ability to communicate clearly to them the ideas and directions that You have given me. Help them to understand the decisions that are being made which involve them. Help me to be open to their input in these matters.

Lord, grant me the wisdom to balance the tangible, strategic and tactical aspects of every decision with the intangible, sensitive and human aspects involved in it. Cause me to see my employees as people and not merely as workers, and show me how to bring out the best in each of them.

Help me, Father, to teach them truth. Give me the ability to communicate to them clearly what I expect from them. Help me to deal fairly and honestly with them, to praise them when they do well and to correct them when they fail.

Help me, Father, to be able to share insight and constructive criticism with them. Help me to always focus on the performance and never the performers so that even after correction, they still feel encouraged and excited about their work with a full understanding of what needs to be done to change or correct the specific action under review.

I pray for their families, Lord. Bless them financially and physically. Grant them health and wholeness and provide for their needs abundantly.

I ask, Father, that You grant them joy and enthusiasm concerning their work. By Your Spirit, help them to see the big picture of this organization—not just their small parts in it. Give them the ability to understand that the more they put into their work, the more they will derive from it.

Help them, Lord, to control their tongues. Cause them to realize that strife and gossip and backbiting are destructive forces which will, in the end, not only negatively affect the company but, more seriously, destroy them spiritually.

Raise up among their ranks Joshuas and Calebs and make them evident to me. Give me insight on who to promote and where to place them for maximum advantage.

I thank You, Father, for sending us good people—qualified and dedicated men and women to do the jobs that need to be done. I thank You that they are anointed of You. You have said that those You call, You also anoint, and that those You anoint, You also equip. Thank You for Your anointing to get the job done above and beyond our own strengths, abilities, gifts and talents.

Thank You for imparting to all the employees of this company everything they need to perform their duties with joy and excellence. I pray that at the end of the day, they may truthfully say, "I have given my all and done my best." Thank You for Your blessings upon them because of their commitment and their faithfulness to You and this company.

In Jesus' name I pray, amen.

Scripture References

2 Chronicles 35:2 AMP

Psalm 45:1 NIV

1 Timothy 5:21 NIV

James 3:17 AMP

Hebrews 13:21 AMP

Matthew 25:21

1 Peter 2:14 AMP

Proverbs 29:19 AMP

3 John 2 AMP

2 Corinthians 7:4

Luke 6:38 NIV

James 3:2 AMP

2 Corinthians 1:21 AMP

1 John 2:27 AMP

Matthew 25:23 NIV

Hiring a New Employee

Father, I come to You concerning the position that is available in our company. I believe that for every individual You created You have a perfect will and plan and purpose.

Lord, I ask You to send the right person for this job, a person who, at this time in his/her life, is Your perfect choice to fill the vacant position in our midst.

If such an individual is already working in this organization and we need to promote him/her, thank You for revealing it to that person and to us. If that perfect someone is not currently employed by our company, then draw that individual here.

Father, if the right person is somebody who doesn't quite match up to our expectations but within whose heart You have placed the potential to be all that we need, please reveal that fact to our hearts. If someone applies with all the natural abilities and talents needed for the job, but whose heart is not right, or for whom the position is not right, put a check in our spirits so that we might know that this is not the person You have chosen.

Father, in 2 Chronicles 22:15 You told Solomon that You would send him workmen who were talented and cunning for every manner of work. We seek someone who has the right gifts and talents for this job, but we also seek someone with the right character and personality, the right personal attributes. We seek someone who has a spirit and attitude that are pleasing to You; someone whose character, integrity and morality are above reproach; someone who will be an outstanding employee and an excellent co-worker; someone who is willing to accept responsibility and take on new challenges; someone who will be a great leader; someone who will rise to the occasion; someone who is committed and faithful to give his/her best to whatever he/she does.

Thank You for an individual who will be supportive of those in positions of leadership and will pray for and submit to them.

Lord, we do not want anyone who is interested in building his/her own kingdom or anyone whose ego is bigger than his/her heart. We want people who are interested in building Your Kingdom and who know how to submit and follow, yet maintain their own independence. We want self-starters and self-motivators.

Father, we seek an individual who is not too proud to be humble nor too timid to stand up for what is right. Send us a thinker. Send us someone who is teachable and eager to learn and to take up new duties and responsibilities.

I thank You, Lord, that in the interview process You will reveal to us the precise individual for the position that is open.

Father, not our will, but Your will be done. I thank You for sending just the perfect individual, called and anointed of You, to fill this position.

In Jesus' name I pray, amen.

Scripture References

Jeremiah 29:11	Proverbs 21:5
Romans 8:28	Luke 9:62
Daniel 1:17	1 Timothy 2:1-3
Daniel 9:22	Ephesians 5:21,22
Psalm 25:21	1 Peter 3:8
Proverbs 12:3	1 John 2:27
Proverbs 19:1	

PRAYER FOR A NEW EMPLOYEE

Father, I thank You for _____, whom
we have just hired as a new employee for our company.
Lord, I believe that we have heard Your voice and that
this is the right choice. I ask You to help him/her to
become comfortable in his/her new position. Thank
You for his/her learning curve, that he/she learns
quickly and rapidly. Give him/her insight and wisdom
concerning his/her new job.

The beginning of a new job is normally a stress-
ful time, but I ask that Your peace, which passes all

understanding, will engulf and surround this individual—that the stress of starting a new job and learning new things and meeting new people will be eliminated and that this will be a joyful and exciting time for all concerned.

Father, I pray for those who will train this new employee. I thank You that You give them wisdom and understanding about what to say and how to say it. Help them to know how to give proper instructions. Help them to be sensitive to this new individual as they work together as a team.

Father, I pray that through this transition period whatever needs to be said will be said, and whatever examples need to be given will be given and that it will be an efficient and effective time of training for all concerned.

Help this new employee to feel loved and well-received by all who work here. I ask You to help other employees in the company to extend their expressions of kindness and acceptance, so that as soon as possible the new person will feel a part of this organization.

Help him/her to be comfortable here and to feel within his/her heart that he/she is a vital, contributing force to the success of this organization.

In Jesus' name I pray, amen.

Scripture References

Philippians 4:7	Psalm 35:9
2 Corinthians 4:8	Ephesians 1:17
Psalm 25:17	Acts 5:12
Psalm 107:6	Philippians 2:2
Psalm 5:11	Ephesians 1:6

Promoting Someone

Father, I come to You regarding _____.
I believe that his/her attitude, talent, commitment and
performance are what we need in this organization and
are in keeping with the requirements of a new job
opening in the company. For this reason, I feel in my
heart that he/she should fill this position.

Lord, if there is some reason this individual
should not be promoted, I ask You to reveal the
reason to me right now. If that does not happen, Lord,
then I am going to follow after my heart, operating
out of the wisdom that You have given me, and
promote this individual.

I thank You, Father, that in this situation the
person sees clearly why he/she is being promoted.
Help me to praise and reinforce those characteristics
that I find worthy of promotion within him/her. Help
me to make it clear that it is because of his/her attitude, behavior and performance that the promotion

has come, and that there are many more such potential promotions in the future.

I ask, Father, that You help this individual to continue to manifest the same attitude, behavior and performance without getting puffed up with pride. Help him/her not to stop doing that which placed him/her into position to be promoted. Let this experience be a springboard to greater accomplishments, productivity and contributions rather than lesser ones. Help this individual to see that this is not the end but the beginning. Help him/her not to get entangled with the pride or arrogance or any other negative attributes that sometimes come with promotion.

Father, if this promotion means that this employee will be dealing with and/or managing people, help him/her to do so with a tender heart. May he/she never abuse his/her authority over anyone, but rather be sensitive and understanding, realizing that managers and supervisors are servants and not masters.

Help this person, Father, to be attuned to the needs of the people who work with him/her. Help him/her to be a coach and not a tyrant, an encourager and not a dictator. Help me to convey to this individual the importance of this truth, and help him/her to walk in its understanding and in the light of Your Word.

In Jesus' name I pray, amen.

Scripture References

1 Corinthians 4:5 NIV   Romans 12:3 NIV

Romans 8:9 NIV   Galatians 5:1

Psalm 75:6,7 AMP   Mark 10:44

Colossians 3:17   Galatians 5:13

Increasing Productivity for Another

Father, I come to You regarding the work performance of _____. It seems to me that he/she should be more productive.

I ask You, Lord, to help me speak to him/her concerning this issue, and then help him/her to accept the challenge to improve. Help him/her to organize his/her work, to see any potential habits that he/she may have that are not productive and to recognize and correct any relationships that are not contributing to his/her success on the job.

Father, speak to _____. Encourage and strengthen him/her. Give him/her wisdom and knowledge of how to organize his/her day, insight on how to stay focused and determination to stay committed to a job until it's done.

Help him/her, Lord, not to get sidetracked, but to be productive and efficient and effective in all that he/she does.

If there is anything I need to do in order to help him/her, or anything I need to share or bring to light, please speak to me and let me know.

In Jesus' name I pray, amen.

Scripture References

Philemon 6	Proverbs 10:4
1 Peter 4:11 NIV	Proverbs 21:5
2 Samuel 2:7	Proverbs 22:29 NIV
Joshua 1:7	Proverbs 27:23
Psalm 60:12	

Correcting an Employee

Lord, I lift up _____. I know it is a difficult situation for any employee when an indiscretion or mistake has to be brought to the attention of his or her supervisor.

Lord, correction is not a pleasant task. But it is a necessary one. I realize that I would be a poor steward of my responsibilities if correction was needed and I did not take appropriate action.

In addressing this situation, help me to focus my attention on the performance, and not on the performer. Help me to speak plainly and accurately, to be objective and not emotional. I pray that I may address this situation in a straightforward and honest manner. At the same time, Lord, help me to build a peace and a confidence in the employee's mind and heart that I am for him/her 100 percent, that I believe in him/her, that I am here to help him/her—not to tear him/her down, but to build him/her up.

Help me to make it clear what action he/she took that I disapproved of, or what action he/she failed to take that caused me to be disappointed. Then help me to make it clear what action I expect him/her to take to correct the situation.

Father, I ask You to help him/her to be open and sensitive so he/she can see his/her mistake and understand the reason for my correction. Help him/her not to take it as a personal affront or reprimand, but rather as an opportunity to overcome and move forward.

Lord, help me to listen to his/her side of the situation, and if it merits a reassessment or rethinking on my part, help me to have an open mind and take the necessary steps to correct my own position. As I listen to what he/she has to say, help me to be sensitive to his/her needs, to realize that it is an embarrassing situation for him/her just as it is for me.

Prepare our hearts, Lord, before the meeting, that our attitudes may be right, our minds may be clear and our spirits may be one so we can bring a sense of unity and objectivity into the meeting.

I ask You, Lord, that when we meet together You will give him/her clarity of thought and an open heart, that he/she may receive what I have to say and apply it to his/her work situation.

In Jesus' name I pray, amen.

Scripture References

Proverbs 29:19 AMP

Jeremiah 10:24 NIV

Job 5:17 NIV

Proverbs 3:11,12 NIV

Proverbs 1:5

Proverbs 8:33 NIV

Romans 2:4 NIV

Psalm 133:1

Ephesians 4:3 NIV

Dismissing an Employee

Father, I am faced with the unpleasant task of dismissing _____.

Lord, I pray concerning the firing of this individual. I believe in my heart that it is the only option left. We have brought the problem area(s) to the attention of the individual. We have done our best to correct the unsatisfactory situation, yet this person has failed to respond in such a way that we feel is adequate behavioral change. Therefore, it seems that termination is the only alternative.

Lord, if there is anything we have overlooked that would salvage this relationship, please speak to my heart and reveal it to me. If not, then I ask Your help in carrying out my duty, as unpleasant and distasteful as it is for all concerned.

I recognize, Lord, that one of the most difficult parts of my job is to let someone go. I also recognize that it is part of my responsibility and that if I fail to fulfill it, it could be damaging to the company, the department and those who work with this individual— even to the person himself/herself.

Therefore, as a good steward of that which You have entrusted to me, and in keeping with the wise counsel which I have received, I believe that I have made this decision in the best interests of the company and of all concerned, including _____.

Give me wisdom that I may be straightforward, speaking the truth in love. Thank You that the attributes of gentleness and mercy will enable me to speak words of hope and consolation.

In the name of Jesus, help _____ to deal with his/her feelings of rejection and to recognize that You will make everything—even discontinuation of employment in this company—accommodate itself to Your purpose and plan for his/her life. His/her talents and abilities are valuable, and there is a God-given place where he/she can develop those gifts in fertile ground, becoming more skilled with business adapted to his/her needs and the company's needs.

In our interview, help me to explain clearly and identify accurately the reasons involved in this decision and to make this difficult transaction less burdensome for all of us. Help me to be sensitive to his/her needs and to the awkwardness and precariousness of the situation. Yet, Father, help me to do my job effectively and efficiently as I should.

In Jesus' name I pray, amen.

Scripture References

Psalm 43:3   Galatians 5:22-25
Revelation 3:19 NIV   Lamentations 3:22,23 NIV
Ephesians 4:15   Hebrews 12:5,6 NIV
2 Timothy 2:24 AMP

PRAYER FOR A FIRED EMPLOYEE

I pray for _____ as he/she leaves this place. I regret that it was necessary to terminate his/her employment with our organization, but feel that there was no alternative.

Now, Father, I pray for this person concerning the future. Help him/her, first of all, to overcome any sense of rejection that he/she might feel. I ask that You minister to him/her and reveal Yourself to him/her, that he/she might know that You are our only security and that by Your Spirit You can help him/her through this painful transition.

Father, I ask You to help him/her not to harbor bitterness, because in the end wrong emotions only hurt the person who harbors them. Help him/her to see this experience as clearly and objectively as possible and to overcome any hurt or embarrassment it might cause.

Father, I ask You to help his/her family during this time of difficulty, awkwardness and embarrassment. Abundantly provide for them, financially as well as mentally and socially. I pray that his/her family will be supportive and that all of them will see this as an opportunity, as a springboard and not a stumbling block to their future. I pray that they will not be discouraged or feel rejected because of it, but that they will set out with fresh vigor—hopeful and expectant for the future.

I pray that this experience will be a turnaround in the life of _____. If the reason he/she was fired was bad habit patterns he/she had developed or wrong attitudes that he/she had exhibited, quicken his/her heart, minister to him/her that this termination was correction that needed to be made in him/her so that he/she may go forward and be successful in a new position. If this termination came about because the job was incompatible with his/her talents, abilities or desires, I ask You, Father, to open up a new opportunity for him/her where he/she might be truly happy, fulfilled and productive.

Open doors for him/her that no man can shut, and shut doors that no man can open. Give him/her the ability to hear the voice of the Good Shepherd and to pursue his/her career in an excellent manner to the best of his/her ability. I pray that he/she will be in the best position for his/her growth and development and the good of the company that hires him/her.

Thank You, Lord, in Jesus' name. Amen.

Scripture References

Ephesians 4:31,32 AMP   Revelation 3:7,8 NIV

Hebrews 12:15 AMP   John 10:27

Philippians 4:19   Jeremiah 29:11-14 NIV

3 John 2

Serving Customers

Father, I pray for our customers today. I thank You for them because without them we could not stay in business.

Thank You, Lord, for all those who buy our products or use our services. Help us to be more sensitive to their needs and more responsive to their wants and desires. Help us to serve them better, because it is in serving our customers better that our company grows and prospers.

Help us to be on the lookout for ways to provide better products/services. Show us how we can be more sensitive to the needs of our clients.

Help us, Lord, always to have a hearing ear to what our customers have to say concerning our products/services. Help us to respond quickly and effectively to those areas that they call to our attention.

Father, I pray that our relationship with them, and theirs with us and our products/services, will be a pleasant and memorable one, that it will bring joy and peace to our hearts and theirs. Help us always to remember that in helping to fulfill their needs, desires and wants we are creating a strong, long-lasting relationship between us and them that will profit both of us and be a blessing to many others.

In Jesus' name I pray, amen.

Scripture References

Galatians 5:13	Proverbs 8:12
Psalm 115:14	Proverbs 2:2
Philippians 2:7	Romans 15:13

Lifting Up Vendors

Lord, I lift up our vendors—those organizations and individuals who contribute to the growth and productivity of this company. Help us to have a good relationship with them. Help us to appreciate and acknowledge their efforts on our behalf. Help us to realize that even though we are buying their products and services, it is still a partnership between us and that without them we could not accomplish that which we need to achieve in order to be a successful organization.

Father, I thank You for giving them success, not only in their business dealings with us but in all their dealings both professional and personal. I thank You that they are blessed and prospered because through their dealings with us we are blessed and prospered. Give them wisdom and insight concerning their business, and prosper everything they put their hands to.

Help us to be a witness and a blessing to every one of our vendors. May they see Your favor and Your blessing upon us and realize that any contact they have with us is an encounter with You—an encounter with Your love and goodness, an encounter with Your joy and peace, an encounter with Your abundance.

In Jesus' name I pray, amen.

Scripture References

Deuteronomy 7:13 NIV

Proverbs 16:16

Deuteronomy 28:12

Isaiah 11:2

Psalm 132:15

Colossians 4:5 NIV

Joshua 1:8

John 13:15

3 John 2

1 Timothy 4:12 NIV

Proverbs 10:22

Psalm 5:12

Part III

*S*pecial
Prayers
for Employees

Prayer of Commitment to Employer

As an employee, I consider myself a team member yoked together with my employer and co-workers. Gladly, I assume my share of the workload and set my heart to serve others. I consider my employer worthy of full respect, so that God's name and His teachings may not be slandered. It will never be truly said that I am a poor worker.

I agree to the sound instruction of my Lord Jesus Christ and to godly teaching. I refuse to quibble over the meaning of Christ's words and to stir up arguments ending in jealousy and anger, which only lead to name-calling, accusations and evil suspicions. I will tell the truth at all times.

Godliness with contentment is great gain. For I brought nothing into the world, and I can take nothing out of it. I have food and clothing, and I am content with that.

I understand that the love of money is a root of all kinds of evil. My motive for working is not to get rich. I would not wander from the faith and pierce myself with many griefs. Instead, I work that I may have something to share with those in need.

I set aside hidden agendas and factional motives. In the true spirit of humility, I regard others as better than and superior to myself [thinking more highly of others than I do of myself.] I esteem my employer and co-workers and look upon and am concerned for their interests as well as my own. I allow the same attitude and purpose and [humble] mind to be in me which was in Christ Jesus: [He is my example in humility].

Thank You, Father, for creating in me a servant's heart and attitude.

In Jesus' name I pray, amen.

Scripture References

1 Timothy 6:1-10 NIV   Ephesians 4:28 NIV
1 Timothy 6:1-10 TLB   Philippians 2:3-5 AMP

Prayer of Daily Dedication to Service

Father, I thank You and praise You for this day. I dedicate myself, afresh and anew, to You and to Your service. I commit to live and operate today according to Your Word and the principles and precepts that You have established in it.

I place myself in Your hands. I submit my will to Your will. In Your Word You have promised that You will give me wisdom in the affairs of life. I receive Your wisdom in every decision I make. Help me to consider both sides of every issue, to see all the facts involved in every situation and to think clearly and accurately.

When I encounter situations or become involved in circumstances beyond my knowledge or experience, I will yield to the Holy Spirit, Whom You have sent to reveal to me all things. I will ask Him to minister to me, to lead me, guide me and direct me in the truth concerning every matter that I have to deal with today.

I choose by an act of my will to be the very best employee that I can be this day, to give my employer 100 percent of my time, my effort and my loyalty.

Father, according to Your Word, everything that I set my hand to shall prosper. I thank You, Lord, that my work shall prosper today. Show me mistakes before they occur and reveal to me how to be more effective and efficient in my work. Help me to bring glory and honor to You in every action I take, every deed I perform and every word I speak.

Thank You that my mind is active and alert. I put out of my thoughts all my personal concerns, and I focus totally on the work before me, giving full attention to the duties and responsibilities that have been assigned me this day.

I thank You that my enthusiasm for my job will be evident to all concerned, and that the excellent way I perform my duties will be a witness to everyone who comes in contact with me.

I choose to be patient and kind to all those who work with me. Thank You that the faithful shall abound in blessings. No matter what the situation, regardless of the circumstances, I will respond in love and in truth. I will not seek my own way or try to promote myself, but I will be secure in the knowledge that if I am faithful and diligent to do my job to the best of my ability, then recognition and promotion will come—from You.

I refuse to lift up myself, to try to force myself into a position of prominence so that others will notice me. I simply commit myself to do whatever I have been assigned to do with all my strength and might and heart and soul.

Thank You that my honest efforts and godly attitude will become obvious to my superiors so that pay increases and promotions will follow as a matter of course. Help me always to be on the lookout for ways to increase my contribution to the success of my department and the company as a whole. In this way, I will find favor with You and with others.

In Jesus' name I pray, amen.

Scripture References

Psalm 118:24

Proverbs 4:20-22 AMP

James 4:7

Proverbs 2:7

John 16:13

Deuteronomy 28:12

1 Corinthians 2:16

Romans 12:2

2 Timothy 2:24 NIV

Proverbs 10:22

Psalm 75:6,7

Ephesians 6:10

Psalm 5:12

Prayer for the Company

Father, I pray for _____ today. I thank You for this organization and for the opportunity to be a part of it. I am grateful for the chance to earn the income this firm provides for me and my family and for the blessing that it has been to me and all its employees.

Father, I thank You that _____ enjoys a good reputation, that it is seen well in the minds of its customers and vendors. Thank You that it prospers and makes a profit, that You give it favor with its clients, that You continue to provide wisdom and insight to those within it who occupy important decision-making positions.

It is my prayer that _____ will continue to thrive and prosper. Thank You for increased sales and expanded markets.

Thank You, Father, for the creativity that is evident in the different areas of the company—new product ideas and new servicing concepts—innovations and techniques that keep this organization vibrant, alive and thriving.

I ask You, Lord, to bless it and to cause it to be a blessing to the market it serves, as well as to all those whose lives are invested in it on a daily basis.

In Jesus' name I pray, amen.

Scripture References

1 Timothy 2:1-3	Proverbs 3:21
3 John 2	Psalm 115:14
Joshua 1:8	Proverbs 8:12
Psalm 5:12	Malachi 3:12 AMP
Proverbs 2:7	Hebrews 6:14

Prayer for Company Executives

Father, in the name of Jesus, I thank You for the privilege of serving You as an employee here at _____. I ask You to send Your Holy Spirit to teach me to pray for the good of the company, that Your name may be glorified.

I pray for those who are in positions of authority and leadership in it. I offer this prayer on behalf of the company executives, asking that You turn their hearts in the way that You would have them go.

I pray for the president and other officers, thanking You for their commitment and dedication to this organization. Thank You that they are upright and honest in all their business dealings. Thank You for providing them new and creative ideas on how to better fulfill their duties and responsibilities and complete the tasks that You have entrusted to them.

Give them insight and understanding beyond their reason. Thank You for Your anointing upon them that goes far beyond their natural gifts and talents. Give them, I pray, clear and distinct direction so that they know what to do and how to do it. Grant them the vision to develop new ideas and concepts and the ability to implement them for the good of all concerned.

Help them, Father, to be sensitive to the needs of every individual in this company. Give them the ability to balance the financial and human resources available to them. Give them supernatural foresight and discernment concerning personnel matters.

Thank You, Father, that they receive all the pertinent information necessary to make good and correct decisions. Help me to be a blessing to them, to respect them and to give honor where honor is due. May I always be an asset to them and never a liability.

Thank You that when we pray in obedience to Your will for those who occupy positions of authority or high responsibility, outwardly, we will experience a quiet and undisturbed life and, inwardly, a peaceable one in all godliness and reverence and seriousness in every way.

During these days of constant change, help those in authority to maintain a positive attitude and to count it all joy when they fall into various trails, knowing that the testing of their faith produces patience. Help them to remember that patience is a force that will enable them to persevere.

In the name of Jesus, I command the spirit of fear to be far from the owners and directors of this organization. Clothed in the armor of God, I stand against any pressure and anxiety that would cause them to make hasty or unwise decisions. Help them to discern between good and bad choices and to make wise decisions—decisions that will contribute to the growth of this company and work for the benefit of every employee.

In Jesus' name I pray, amen.

Scripture References

2 Thessalonians 1:12   1 Timothy 2:1-3

Proverbs 21:1   Isaiah 33:6

Psalm 25:21   James 1:2-4

Romans 12:17 NIV   Hebrews 10:35,36

Ephesians 1:9,17   2 Timothy 1:7

Proverbs 3:5,6   Ephesians 6:11-18

Psalm 37:23 AMP

Prayer for a Superior

Father, in Your Word, You said to pray for those who exercise authority over us, so I pray for my manager/supervisor today. I ask You to give him/her clarity of thought concerning every decision made this day. Help him/her to clearly identify and accurately assess every potential problem. Help him/her to make the right decisions—to respond, and not to react, to whatever situation or circumstance might arise during the course of the day.

I ask You, Father, to help him/her to set the proper priorities today. Reveal to him/her what tasks are most important and cause him/her to inspire us to perform our duties to the best of our abilities.

I ask that You help him/her to be sensitive to the needs of those under his/her supervision, those who work for him/her. Help him/her to realize that not everyone is the same and that no two people respond or react in the same way. Help him/her to adapt his/her management style or technique to the strengths, weaknesses and personality type of each individual. Grant him/her the ability to manage beyond his/her own natural gifts and talents. I pray that he/she will rely upon You, drawing strength, wisdom and insight from You.

I purpose in my heart to set a guard over my mouth. I refuse to say anything negative or disrespectful about my manager/supervisor. I choose to support him/her and to say only good things about him/her.

Lord, I ask You to give him/her a peaceful spirit, so that even in the midst of great turmoil he/she may act with surety and confidence and make wise decisions. Help me to be sensitive to his/her needs and responsibilities. Show me ways, Lord, to support him/her and to assist him/her in the performance of his/her duties.

Father, You have said in Your Word that Your Spirit will show us things to come. I ask You to show my manager/supervisor the solution to small problems before they become major problems. Grant him/her creative ideas on how he/she can better lead and manage his/her department.

For all these things I give You thanks, praise and glory, in Jesus' name. Amen.

Scripture References

1 Timothy 2:1-3 AMP	Isaiah 40:29-31 AMP
1 Corinthians 2:16	Philippians 4:7
Ephesians 4:23,24	Hebrews 12:14
Matthew 6:33 AMP	John 14:26
Romans 12:10	John 16:13

Prayer for Self

Lord, help me today to do my very best. I give myself 100 percent to my company. Help me to be the most valuable worker possible, one who is sensitive to the needs of his co-workers and responsive to the desires of his employer. I purpose to perform my duties with a spirit of excellence, to do all that is required of me, and even above and beyond that which is required of me, that I may be a blessing to others and an asset to this company.

Lord, I purpose in my heart to fulfill my duties to the best of my ability. I vow never to shirk my responsibilities or to be slack in my work. If I make a mistake, I will be open and honest and forthright, admitting it and doing all I can to correct it.

I make a commitment not to try to impress anybody but to do my job humbly and quietly, effectively and efficiently. I will not stretch the truth or give the impression that something is true when it's not. I will not be lax or lazy but will be conscientious and trust-worthy in all my business dealings.

I will do my best to establish and maintain good relationships with my co-workers and superiors. I am committed to be a faithful, devoted worker. Whatever my hand touches, that I will do with all my might, with all my energy, with all that is within me. I will do everything in my power to become the most produc-tive employee in this organization. I solemnly pledge that I will be nothing but a blessing to it.

I know, Lord, that promotion comes from You. I thank You that the faithful will be rewarded and that I will abound in blessings. Thank You that my attitude, commitment and performance on the job will become obvious to those for whom I work and that recogni-tion, promotion, benefits and raises will follow as a matter of course.

Thank You for the opportunity to see You show Yourself strong on my behalf. I call upon the Greater One Who is in me today to provide me strength, knowledge, wisdom and ability beyond my human limits. Thank You that I operate supernaturally today, by the power of Your indwelling Spirit so that I am able to perform my duties with outstanding accuracy and excellence.

In Jesus' name I pray, amen.

Scripture References

Proverbs 16:3 NIV   Colossians 3:17

Daniel 5:12 AMP   Proverbs 28:20

Proverbs 17:27 AMP   2 Chronicles 16:9

Proverbs 10:4   1 John 4:4

Proverbs 22:29 NIV   Psalm 75:6,7

Romans 12:17 NIV

Prayer for an Increase in Personal Productivity

Father, I come to You out of frustration because I am not pleased with my performance on the job. It seems that I am not producing that which I should be producing because I am just not as efficient or effective as I need to be.

Lord, I ask for Your help in planning my day, paying attention to my duties, staying focused on my assignment, establishing priorities in my work and making steady progress toward my objectives.

Give me insight, Father. Help me to see any habits that I may have that might tend to make me unproductive. Reveal to me ways to better handle the tedious tasks I must perform, so that I can achieve the greatest results possible. Help me to organize my efforts, schedule my activities and budget my time.

From books, by Your Spirit, through the people who work with me or by whatever means You choose,

Lord, reveal to me that which I need to know and do in order to become a more productive, fruitful worker.

My heart's desire is to give my very best to You and to my employer. When I become frustrated because that is not taking place, help me, Father, by the power of Your Spirit to do whatever is necessary to correct that situation so that I can once again function with accuracy and proficiency.

Thank You, Lord, for bringing all these things to pass in my life.

In Jesus' name I pray, amen.

Scripture References

Psalm 118:24   Psalm 119:99 AMP

Proverbs 16:9 AMP   Proverbs 9:10 AMP

Proverbs 19:21 AMP   1 Corinthians 4:5

Ephesians 1:17

Prayer When Persecuted at Work

Father, I come to You in the name that is above all other names—the name of Jesus. Your name is a strong tower that I can run into and be safe when I am persecuted on the job.

Lord, I admit that these unkind words really hurt me. I desire to be accepted by my boss and co-workers, but I long to obey You and follow Your commandments. I know that Jesus was tempted just as I am, but He didn't give in to sin or hate. Please give me Your mercy and grace to deal with this situation. I look to You for my comfort; You are a true Friend at all times.

Thank You, Lord, for never leaving me alone or rejecting me. I make a decision to forgive the people who have spoken unkind words about me. I ask You to work this forgiveness in my heart. I submit to You and reject the disappointment and anger that have attempted to consume me. Specifically right now I forgive _____.

I ask You to cause this situation to accommodate itself for good in my life. **To you, O Lord, I lift up my soul; in You I trust, O my God. Do not let me be put to shame, nor let my enemies triumph over me** (Ps. 25:1,2 NIV).

Because I love You, O Lord, You will rescue me; You will protect me because I acknowledge Your name. I will call upon You, and You will deliver me; You will be with me in trouble; You will deliver me and honor me.

Father, I will resist the temptation to strike back in anger. I purpose to love _____ with the love of Jesus in me. Mercy and truth are written upon the tablets of my heart; therefore, You will cause me to find favor and understanding with my boss and co-workers. Keep me from self-righteousness so that I may walk in Your righteousness. Thank You for sending and giving me friends who will stand by me and teach me how to guard my heart with all diligence.

I declare that in the midst of all these things I am more than a conqueror through Jesus, Who loves me. I can use the witty inventions You have provided me, and I will be confident in Your wisdom when working. I am of good courage and pray that freedom of utterance be given to me as I do my job.

In Jesus' name I pray, amen.

Scripture References

Philippians 2:9	Proverbs 3:3,4
Proverbs 18:10	Proverbs 4:23
Hebrews 4:15	Romans 8:37
Proverbs 17:17	Proverbs 8:12
Hebrews 13:5	Psalm 31:24
Proverbs 16:4 AMP	Ephesians 6:19
Psalm 91:14,15 NIV	

Prayer When Passed Over for Promotion

Father, in the name of Jesus I come before Your throne of grace to receive appropriate and well-timed help. I feel that my employer has been unfair to me in the recent changes within the company. Another person has been promoted to the position for which I aspire and even now believe I rightfully deserve.

I cannot change this situation, so I look to You to help me overcome anger and disappointment. Forgive me for the accusations I have made against my boss. I come to You in repentance, casting down every high and lofty thought that sets itself up against the knowledge of You.

Lord, it is You Who give me more and more grace (power of the Holy Spirit, to meet this evil tendency—these thoughts of self-aggrandizement and pride—and all others fully). I choose by my noble living to show forth my [good] works with (unobtrusive) humility [which is the proper attribute] of true wisdom.

Your Word says to rejoice with those who rejoice, so I rejoice with the person who has been promoted. I realize, Lord, that this individual would not have received this promotion if he/she had not deserved it.

I put my own feelings aside and pray for Your richest blessing upon him/her. I refuse to allow a root of bitterness toward this person or the company to spring up in my heart and poison my life. I refuse to hold anyone accountable for this situation, but entrust it entirely to You.

Lord, I place my situation, my future, into Your hand, committing, with greater assurance than ever, to do my very best with the gifts and talents You have given me. If there are any bad habits in my work or improper attitudes in my heart that would keep me from being promoted, I ask You to reveal them to me and help me to overcome them.

I will not seek to promote myself, or to bring myself to the attention of people, but I will bring myself to Your attention by doing my job to the best of my ability.

Help me to write love and faithfulness upon the tablets of my heart. Then I will win favor and a good name in the sight of God and man. I choose to trust in You with all my heart and lean not on my own understanding; in all my ways I acknowledge You, and You will make my paths straight.

I refuse the pressure to make a hasty decision, remembering that the plans of the diligent lead to profit as surely as haste leads to poverty.

You are my help in this time of distress, and with the help of the Holy Spirit I humble myself [feeling very insignificant] in Your presence, and You will exalt me. [You will lift me up and make my life significant.]

Father, I look to You for appropriate and well-timed promotions. For not from the east, nor from the west, nor from the south come promotion and lifting up, but from You, Lord, the righteous Judge!

In Jesus' name I pray, amen.

Scripture References

Hebrews 4:16 AMP   Hebrews 12:15

2 Corinthians 10:5   Proverbs 3:3-6 NIV

James 4:6 AMP   Proverbs 21:5 NIV

James 3:13 AMP   James 4:10 AMP

Romans 12:15   Psalm 75:6

Prayer at Quitting Time

Father, I thank You for this day. Now I step out of the role of employee and into the role of husband and father/mother and wife.

Lord, I thank You that I do not carry the baggage of the day home with me, but I leave it at the office. Whatever responsibilities, problems or situations I had to face there, however difficult the day may have been for me, I give it all to You. By an act of my will, I choose not to think about it, meditate on it or allow it to control my life.

With the same zeal, enthusiasm and fervor that I started this day, I now turn toward home. My spouse and children deserve a husband and father/wife and mother who is happy to see them, someone who is filled with energy, happiness and joy. I refuse to drag across the threshold weary, worn out and beaten down by the day's activities.

Father, grant me a refreshing now, for the second part of my day. Thank You that Your joy overflows in my heart so that I come home as a solution, not a problem. As I enter the doorway, let me bring with me joy and peace and life, not misery, frustration and fatigue.

Lord, I ask You to strengthen me: spirit, soul and body. Fill my heart with Your love and grace. Clear my mind of the cobwebs of the day. Thank You that I can choose to put a smile on my face and joy in my heart, that I can determine in advance to have a wonderful evening with my family. Thank You that I can bring with me the character and personality of one who is in love with You and in love with his/her spouse and children.

Lord, help me to be sensitive to the needs of my mate. Help me to listen as he/she tells me about his/her day. Help me to be excited with him/her in his/her moments of triumph, to be sympathetic with him/her in his/her moments of stress and anxiety. I understand that there is no harder work or more difficult job than balancing the daily demands of life and the raising of and providing for young children.

Help me to be sensitive to the needs of my spouse. Help me to express to him/her that I do value his/her contribution to the family, that I do love him/her and appreciate everything he/she does for me and for our children.

Lord, help me never—under any circumstances, either by word or deed—to be condescending or to insinuate that I think less of his/her responsibilities than I do my own or that I consider them in any way subordinate to mine. Help me to encourage and strengthen him/her, to be his/her best friend and closest confidant.

Lord, I know that no one has the influence over our children's lives that my spouse and I do. Help me to be that role model that they need as a parent. Thank You for physical strength in my body so I can play with my children in the evening. Thank You for clarity of mind so I can be sensitive to their conversations and attuned to the events of their day. Help me not to consider the details of their lives and their daily activities trivial, but help me to see things from their perspectives and viewpoints.

Lord, help me to respond with excitement and enthusiasm to whatever made them happy today. Help me to be tenderhearted and sympathetic to whatever challenges they had to face in their world today. Help me, Lord, to instill within them a confidence, a trust and surety in You, and a dependence upon You.

Help me to present what I do in such a way that they never resent my work but realize that my job is a gift from You and that through it You bless our family so that it is a positive contribution to our lives.

Help me never to speak ill about anyone in my work place, or say anything that will give my family wrong thoughts or ideas or attitudes toward my work. Help me to be a full-time spouse and a full-time parent this entire evening. Thank You for the gift of Your Holy Spirit to empower me for the work You have called me to do and to fulfill the role at home that You have entrusted to me.

In Jesus' name I pray, amen.

Scripture References

Psalm 19:14	Joel 3:10
Psalm 28:7	Ephesians 4:32
Proverbs 17:22	1 Timothy 4:14
Isaiah 40:29 NIV	Proverbs 15:23 AMP
Isaiah 41:10 AMP	Romans 13:10 AMP
Psalm 127:3-5	Acts 1:8

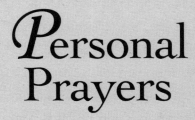

Part IV

Personal Prayers

To Walk in the Word

Father, in the name of Jesus, *I commit myself to walk in the Word.* Your Word living in me produces Your life in this world. I recognize that Your Word is integrity itself—steadfast, sure, eternal—and I trust my life to its provisions.

You have sent your Word forth into my heart. I let it dwell in me richly in all wisdom. I meditate in it day and night so that I may diligently act on it. The Incorruptible Seed, the Living Word, the Word of Truth, is abiding in my spirit. That Seed is growing mightily in me now, producing Your nature, Your life. It is my counsel, my shield, my buckler, my powerful weapon in battle. The Word is a lamp to my feet and a light to my path. It makes my way plain before me. I do not stumble, for my steps are ordered in the Word.

The Holy Spirit leads and guides me into all the truth. He gives me understanding, discernment and comprehension so that I am preserved from the snares of the evil one.

I delight myself in You and Your Word. Because of that, You put Your desires within my heart. I commit my way unto You, and You bring it to pass. I am confident that You are at work in me now both to will and to do all Your good pleasure.

I exalt Your Word, hold it in high esteem and give it first place. *I make my schedule around Your Word.* I make the Word final authority to settle all questions that confront me. I choose to agree with the Word of God, and I choose to disagree with any thoughts, conditions or circumstances contrary to Your Word. I boldly and confidently say that my heart is fixed and established on the solid foundation—the living Word of God!

Scripture References

Hebrews 4:12	1 Peter 3:12
Colossians 3:16	Colossians 4:2
Joshua 1:8	Ephesians 6:10
1 Peter 1:23	Luke 18:1
Psalm 91:4	James 5:16
Psalm 119:105	Psalm 37:4,5
Psalm 37:23	Philippians 2:13
Colossians 1:9	2 Corinthians 10:5
John 16:13	Psalm 112:7,8

To Rejoice in the Lord

Father, this is the day You have made. I rejoice and am glad in it! I rejoice in You always. And again I say, I rejoice. I delight myself in You, Lord. Happy am I because God is my Lord!

Father, thank You for loving me and rejoicing over me with joy. Hallelujah! I am redeemed. I come with singing, and everlasting joy is upon my head. I obtain joy and gladness, and sorrow and sighing flee away. That spirit of rejoicing, joy and laughter is my heritage. Where the Spirit of the Lord is there is liberty—emancipation from bondage, freedom. I walk in that liberty.

Father, I praise You with joyful lips. I am ever filled and stimulated with the Holy Spirit. I speak out in psalms and hymns and make melody with all my heart to You, Lord. My happy heart is a good medicine, and my cheerful mind works healing. The light in my eyes rejoices the hearts of others. I have a good report. My countenance radiates the joy of the Lord.

Father, I thank You that I bear much prayer fruit. I ask in Jesus' name, and I will receive so that my joy (gladness, delight) may be full, complete and overflowing. The joy of the Lord is my *strength*. Therefore, I count it all joy, all strength, when I encounter tests or trials of any sort, because I am strong in You, Father.

I have the *victory* in the name of Jesus. Satan is under my feet. I am not moved by adverse circumstances. I have been made the righteousness of God in Christ Jesus. I dwell in the Kingdom of God and have peace and joy in the Holy Spirit! Praise the Lord!

Scripture References

Psalm 118:24	Philippians 4:8
Philippians 4:4	Proverbs 15:13
Philippians 3:1	John 15:7,8
Psalm 144:15	John 16:23
Zephaniah 3:17	Nehemiah 8:10
Isaiah 51:11	James 1:2
2 Corinthians 3:17	Ephesians 6:10
James 1:25	1 John 5:4

Psalm 63:5
Ephesians 5:18,19
Proverbs 17:22
Proverbs 15:30

Ephesians 1:22
2 Corinthians 5:7
2 Corinthians 5:21
Romans 14:17

To Have Confidence

Jehovah God, I am Your child. You are my Father. Because Your presence goes with me, I am ready to face each day with its new beginnings. Yesterday is gone. Old things have passed away and, behold, all things have become new; and all things are of You.

Once I was "darkness," but now as a Christian I am "light." I live as a child of the light. The light produces in me all that is good and right and true. I desire for my life to be living proof of the things which please You. Light is capable of showing up everything for what it really is.

I will do all I have to do without grumbling or arguing, so that I may be blameless and harmless, Your faultless child, living in a warped and diseased age, and shining like a light in a dark world.

You, Father, are the Vinedresser; Jesus is the Vine; and I am the branch. I am fruitful in all my work, for I share His life and He shares my life. You always cause me to triumph in Christ Jesus, in Whose name I pray, amen.

Scripture References

2 Corinthians 5:17,18   John 15:1-7 NIV
Ephesians 5:8-11,13 PHILLIPS   2 Corinthians 2:14
Philippians 2:14,15 PHILLIPS

To Exercise Self-Discipline

DEVOTIONAL READING

He who is slow to anger is better than the mighty, he who rules his [own] spirit than he who takes a city.

Proverbs 16:32 AMP

Conquest and self-control within are better than conquest of enemies without.[1]

PRAYER

Father, I desire to be self-disciplined. I affirm that I am maturing in the fruit of the Spirit, which is love, joy, peace, patience, kindness, goodness, faithfulness, gentleness and self-control. Against such things there is no law. I belong to Christ Jesus and have crucified the sinful nature with its passions and desires. Since I live by the Spirit, I will keep in step with the Spirit. I resist and give no place to feelings of conceit, or the temptation to envy and provoke others.

I receive every Scripture, for it is God-breathed (given by Your inspiration) and profitable for instruction, for reproof and conviction of sin, for correction of error and discipline in obedience, [and] for training in righteousness (in holy living, in conformity to Your will in thought, purpose and action). This enables me to be complete and proficient, well fitted and thoroughly equipped for every good work.

Lord, You did not give me a spirit of timidity, but a spirit of power, of love and of self-discipline.

Your divine power has given me everything I need for life and godliness through my knowledge of You, Who called me by Your own glory and goodness. Through these You have given me Your very great and precious promises, so that through them I may participate in the divine nature and escape the corruption in the world caused by evil desire. For this very reason, I make every effort to add to my faith goodness; and to goodness, knowledge; and to knowledge, self-control; and to self-control, perseverance; and to perseverance, godliness; and to godliness, brotherly kindness; and to brotherly kindness, love. For if I possess these qualities in increasing measure, they will keep me from being ineffective and unproductive in my knowledge of my Lord Jesus Christ, in Whose name I pray. Amen.

Scripture References

Galatians 5:23-26 NIV

2 Timothy 1:7 NIV

2 Timothy 3:16,17 AMP

2 Peter 1:3-10 NIV

[1]Dake, Finis—*Dakes' Annotated Reference Bible.* (Lawrenceville: Dake Bible Sales, 1963) p. 653.

To Have Appropriate Self-Esteem

Father, Jesus said that I am to love You with all my heart and with all my soul and with all my mind (intellect). This is the great (most important, principal) and first commandment. And a second is like it: I shall love my neighbor as [I do] myself.

I desire to have appropriate self-esteem, and to receive myself just as You created me.

Father, You love me for who I am. It was You Who created me, and You Who formed me. You have redeemed me [ransomed me by paying a price instead of leaving me a captive of Satan]. You have called me by my name. You have said that I am Yours. Before You formed me in the womb You knew and approved of me [as Your chosen instrument], and before I was born You separated and set me apart, consecrating me; [and] You appointed me for a special work. You know me by name, and I have also found favor in Your sight.

I rate my ability with sober judgment, according to the degree of faith apportioned by You to me. As in one physical body we have many parts (organs, members) and all of these parts do not have the same function or use, so we are one body in Christ and individually we are parts one of another [mutually dependent on one another]. Thank You for giving to me gifts (faculties, talents, qualities) that are different and unique according to the grace given me. I will develop and use them.

I face my fears of inadequacy, failure and rejection, knowing that perfect love casts out fear. You created my inmost being. You knit me together in my mother's womb. I praise You because I am fearfully and wonderfully made. Your works are wonderful; I know that full well. I accept myself because You have received, welcomed and accepted me in the Beloved.

In Jesus' name I pray, amen.

Scripture References

Matthew 22:37-39 AMP   Romans 12:3-6 AMP

Isaiah 43:1 AMP   1 John 4:18

Jeremiah 1:5 AMP   Psalm 139:13,14 NIV

Exodus 33:12 AMP   Ephesians 1:6

To Obtain and Maintain Godly Character

Father, I desire to receive wisdom and discipline. I ask for the ability to understand words of insight. By Your grace, I am acquiring a disciplined and prudent life, doing what is right and just and fair.

Thank You for giving me prudence, knowledge and discretion. As a wise person I listen and add to my learning, and as a discerning person I accept guidance [so that I may be able to steer my course rightly].

Thank You that I understand proverbs and parables, the sayings and riddles of the wise.

In Jesus' name I pray, amen.

Scripture References

Proverbs 1:2-7 NIV   Proverbs 1:5 AMP

To Be Well-Balanced

Father, in the name of Jesus, I come boldly to Your throne of grace to receive mercy and find grace to help in time of need.

Forgive me for getting caught up in my own pride. Sometimes I behave as though I am indispensable at home, at the office, at church and in other situations. I become irritable and fatigued, feeling that no one appreciates all that I do. Help me to step back and take a personal inventory. My spirit is Your candle, searching out all the inward parts of my being.

Jesus said, **Come to me, all of you who are weary and over-burdened, and I will give you rest! Put on my yoke and learn from me. For I am gentle and humble in heart and you will find rest for your souls. For my yoke is easy and my burden is light** (Matt. 11:28-30 PHILLIPS).

Lord, not only am I yoked up with You, but also with my spouse, my colleagues and others whom You have sent into my life. I am not alone, and I cannot carry this alone. Help me to resist the temptation to be yoked together with unbelievers for the sake of financial profit.

There is a time for everything, and a season for every activity under heaven. Help me to keep my priorities in order. Help me to fulfill my call and responsibilities at home as a husband/wife and/or parent. While I am at work, help me to stay focused. Also, help me to take time to find rest—relief, ease and refreshment and recreation and blessed quiet—for my soul.

I cast the whole of my care [all my anxieties, all my worries, all my concerns, once and for all] on You, for You care for me affectionately and care about me watchfully. I affirm that I am well-balanced (temperate, sober of mind), vigilant and cautious at all times; for that enemy of mine, the devil, roams around like a lion roaring [in fierce hunger], seeking someone to seize upon and devour. In the name of Jesus, I withstand him; firm in faith [against his onset—rooted, established, strong, immovable and determined]. And after I have suffered a little while, You, the God of all grace [Who imparts all blessing and favor], Who has called me to His [own] eternal glory in Christ Jesus, will Yourself complete and make me what I ought to be, establish and ground me securely, and strengthen and settle me.

To You be the dominion (power, authority, rule) for ever and ever.

Amen (so be it).

Scripture References

Hebrews 4:16	Ecclesiastes 3:1 NIV
Proverbs 20:27	Matthew 11:29 AMP
2 Corinthians 6:14	1 Peter 5:7-11 AMP

To Please God Rather Than Men

Father, I desire to please You rather than men.
Forgive me for loving the approval and the praise and
the glory that come from men [instead of and] more
than the glory that comes from You. [I value my credit
with You more than credit with men.]

I declare that I am free from the fear of man,
which brings a snare. I lean on, trust in and put my
confidence in You. I am safe and set on high.

I take comfort and am encouraged and confidently
and boldly say, "The Lord is my Helper; I will not be
seized with alarm [I will not fear or dread or be terri-
fied]. What can man do to me?"

Father, just as You sent Jesus, You have sent me.
You are ever with me, for I always seek to do what
pleases You.

In Jesus' name I pray, amen.

Scripture References

John 12:43 AMP   John 17:18 AMP

Proverbs 29:25 AMP   John 8:29 AMP

Hebrews 13:6 AMP

To Receive Jesus as Savior and Lord

Father, it is written in Your Word that if I confess with my mouth that Jesus is Lord and believe in my heart that You have raised Him from the dead, I shall be saved. Therefore, Father, I confess that Jesus is my Lord. I make Him Lord of my life right now. I believe in my heart that You raised Jesus from the dead. I renounce my past life with Satan and close the door to any of his devices.

I thank You for forgiving me of all my sin. Jesus is my Lord, and I am a new creation. Old things have passed away. Now all things become new in Jesus' name. Amen.

Scripture References

John 3:16   John 14:6
John 6:37   Romans 10:9,10
John 10:10b   Romans 10:13
Romans 3:23   Ephesians 2:1-10
2 Corinthians 5:19   2 Corinthians 5:17
John 16:8,9   John 1:12
Romans 5:8   2 Corinthians 5:21

To Receive the Infilling of the Holy Spirit

My heavenly Father, I am Your child, for I believe in my heart that Jesus has been raised from the dead and I have confessed Him as my Lord.

Jesus said, "How much more shall your heavenly Father give the Holy Spirit to those who ask Him." I ask You now in the name of Jesus to fill me with the Holy Spirit. I step into the fullness and power that I desire in the name of Jesus. I confess that I am a Spirit-filled Christian. As I yield my vocal organs, I expect to speak in tongues, for the Spirit gives me utterance in the name of Jesus. Praise the Lord!

Scripture References

John 14:16,17	Acts 10:44-46
Luke 11:13	Acts 19:2,5,6
Acts 1:8	1 Corinthians 14:2-15
Acts 2:4	1 Corinthians 14:18,27
Acts 2:32,33,39	Ephesians 6:18
Acts 8:12-17	Jude 1:20

Introduction

The prayers in this section are designed to help you recognize and overcome certain thought patterns and attitudes which can hinder your success in life.

Often, after we have blamed others for our failures, we are startled to discover the real truth—that we are our own worst enemies. Negative thought patterns produce negative results. Positive thought patterns based on God's Word promote positive results: **As** (a man) **thinketh in his heart, so is he...** (Prov. 23:7).

These prayers are by no means exhaustive in content. By praying them earnestly, you can submit to the transforming power of the Holy Spirit, Who will help you change fatalistic, skeptical perspectives to godly perspectives. You can know that you are God's workmanship and see yourself as He sees you.

Many people try to overcome destructive thought patterns through behavior modification without spiritual transformation. It won't work.

Our thought patterns were formed by our family and educational environments, by society and religious dogmas. We are transformed (changed) by the [entire] renewal of our mind [by its new ideals and its new attitude], so that we may prove [for ourselves] what is the good and acceptable and perfect will of God, even the thing which is good and acceptable and perfect [in His sight for us]. (Rom. 12:2 AMP.) We may learn certain techniques and behaviors of success, but it is the inner change of the heart which is lasting and the most productive.

Identifying destructive thought patterns that control our behavior and attitudes is the first step in pulling down destructive ideas that set themselves up against the knowledge of God. You and I were created to be proactive and successful. Believe and affirm that you are more than a conqueror through Him Who loves you (Rom. 8:37).

To Live Free From Worry

Father, I thank You that I have been delivered from the power of darkness and translated into the Kingdom of Your dear Son. *I commit to live free from worry, in the name of Jesus,* for the law of the Spirit of life in Christ Jesus has made me free from the law of sin and death.

I humble myself under Your mighty hand, that in due time You may exalt me. I cast the whole of my cares *(name them)*—all my anxieties, all my worries, all my concerns, once and for all—on You. You care for me affectionately and care about me watchfully. You sustain me. You will never allow the consistently righteous to be moved—made to slip, fall or fail!

Father, I delight myself in You, and You perfect that which concerns me.

I cast down imaginations (reasonings) and every high thing that exalts itself against the knowledge of You, and bring into captivity every thought to the obedience of Christ. I lay aside every weight and the sin of worry, which does try so easily to beset me. I run with patience the race that is set before me, looking unto Jesus, the author and finisher of my faith.

I thank You, Father, that You are able to keep that which I have committed unto You. I think on (fix my mind on) those things that are true, honest, just, pure, lovely, of good report, virtuous and deserving of praise. I let not my heart be troubled. I abide in Your words, and Your words abide in me. Therefore, Father, I do not forget what manner of person I am. I look into the perfect law of liberty and continue therein, being not a forgetful hearer, but a *doer of the Word* and thus blessed in my doing!

Thank You, Father, *I am carefree.* I walk in that peace which passes all understanding, in Jesus' name!

Scripture References

Colossians 1:13	Hebrews 12:1,2
Romans 8:2	2 Timothy 1:12
1 Peter 5:6,7	Philippians 4:8
Psalm 55:22	John 14:1
Psalm 138:8	James 1:22-25
2 Corinthians 10:5	Philippians 4:6

Prosperity

Father, I come to You, in the name of Jesus, concerning my financial situation. You are a very present help in trouble, and You are more than enough. Your Word declares that You shall supply all my need according to Your riches in glory by Christ Jesus.

(If you have not been giving tithes and offerings, include this statement of repentance in your prayer.) Forgive me for robbing You in tithes and offerings. I repent and purpose to bring all my tithes into the storehouse, that there may be food in Your house. Thank You for wise financial counselors and teachers who are teaching me the principles of good stewardship.

Lord of hosts, You said, "Try Me now in this, and I will open the windows of heaven and pour out for you such blessing that there will not be room enough to receive it." You will rebuke the devourer for my sake. My heart is filled with thanksgiving.

Lord, my God, I shall remember that it is You Who give me the power to get wealth, that You may establish Your covenant. In the name of Jesus, I worship You only, and I will have no other gods before me.

You are able to make all grace—every favor and earthly blessing—come to me in abundance, so that I am always, and in all circumstances, furnished in abundance for every good work and charitable donation. Amen.

Scripture References

Psalm 56:1

Philippians 4:19

Malachi 3:8-12

Deuteronomy 8:18-19

2 Corinthians 9:8 AMP

Health and Healing

Father, in the name of Jesus, I come before You asking You to heal me. It is written that the prayer of faith will save the sick, and the Lord will raise him up. And if I have committed sins, I will be forgiven. I let go of all unforgiveness, resentment, anger and bad feelings toward anyone.

My body is the temple of the Holy Spirit, and I desire to be in good health. I seek that which will make me free—both spiritual *(Your Word)* and natural *(good eating habits, medications if necessary, and appropriate rest and exercise)*. You bought me at a price, and I desire to glorify You in my spirit and my body—they both belong to You.

Thank You, Father, for sending Your Word to heal me and deliver me from all my destruction. Jesus, You are the Word who became flesh and dwelt among us. You bore my griefs (pains) and carried my sorrows (sickness). You were pierced through for my transgressions and crushed for my iniquities. The chastening for my well being fell upon You, and by Your scourging I am healed.

Father, I give attention to Your words and incline my ear to Your sayings. I will not let them depart from my sight but will keep them in the midst of my heart, for they are my life and health to my whole body.

Since the Spirit of Him Who raised Jesus from the dead dwells in me, He Who raised Christ from the dead will also give life to my mortal body through His Spirit, Who dwells in me.

Thank You that I will prosper and be in health, even as my soul prospers. Amen.

Scripture References

James 5:15 NKJV	Proverbs 4:21-22 NAS
1 Corinthians 6:19-20	Psalm 103:3-5 NAS
Psalm 107:20	Romans 8:11 NKJV
John 1:14	3 John 2
Isaiah 53:4-5 NAS	

Victory Over Fear

Father, when I am afraid, I will put my confidence in You. Yes, I will trust Your promises. And since I trust You, what can mere man do to me?

You have not given me a spirit of timidity, but of power and love and discipline (sound judgment). Therefore I am not ashamed of the testimony of my Lord. I have not received a spirit of slavery leading to fear again, but I have received a spirit of adoption as a son, by which I cry out, "Abba! Father!"

Jesus, You delivered me, who through fear of death had been living all my life as a slave to constant dread. I receive the gift You left to me—peace of mind and heart! And the peace You give isn't fragile like the peace the world gives. I cast away troubled thoughts, and I choose not to be afraid. I believe in God; I believe also in You.

Lord, You are my light and my salvation, You protect me from danger—whom shall I fear? When evil men come to destroy me, they will stumble and fall! Yes, though a mighty army marches against me, my heart shall know no fear! I am confident that You will save me.

Thank You, Holy Spirit, for bringing these things to my remembrance when I am tempted to be afraid. I will trust in my God. In the name of Jesus, I pray.

Scripture References

Psalm 56:3-5 TLB   Hebrews 2:15 TLB

2 Timothy 1:7-8 NAS   John 14:1,17 TLB

Romans 8:15 NAS   Psalm 27:1-3 TLB

Overcoming Impatience

Father, in the name of Jesus, I thank You for the Holy Spirit, Who helps me develop and exercise patience, a fruit of the Spirit. I will remember that the end of a matter is better than its beginning, and patience is better than pride. I resist the temptation to be quickly provoked in my spirit, for anger resides in the lap of fools.

I desire to live wisely with a due sense of responsibility, as one who knows the meaning and purpose of life. I purpose to make the best use of my time, despite all the difficulties of these days.

I choose to count it all joy when I fall into various trials, knowing that the testing of my faith produces patience. I realize that these come to test my faith and to produce in me the quality of endurance. I purpose to let the process go on until that endurance is fully developed, and I will find that I have become a person of mature character with the right sort of independence.

Father, Your grace (Your favor and loving-kindness and mercy) is enough for me [sufficient against
any danger and enables me to bear trouble manfully];
for Your strength and power are made perfect (fulfilled
and completed) and show themselves most effective in
[my] weakness.

And if, in the process, I do not know how to meet
any particular problem, I ask You, Father—Who give
generously to all men without making them feel
guilty—and I am quite sure that the necessary wisdom
will be given me.

As I live this new life, I pray that I will be
strengthened from Your glorious power, so that I will
find myself able to pass through any experience and
endure it with joy.

In Jesus' name I pray, amen.

Scripture References

Ecclesiastes 7:8,9 NIV   2 Corinthians 12:9 AMP

Ephesians 5:15 PHILLIPS   James 1:3-5 PHILLIPS

James 1:2,3 NKJV   Colossians 1:11 PHILLIPS

Overcoming Intimidation

Father, I come to You in the name of Jesus, confessing that intimidation has caused me to stumble. I ask Your forgiveness for thinking of myself as inferior, for I am created in Your image, and I am Your workmanship. Jesus said that Your Kingdom is within me. Therefore, the power that raised Jesus from the dead dwells in me and causes me to face life with hope and divine energy.

You, Lord, are my light and my salvation; whom shall I fear? You are the strength of my life; of whom shall I be afraid?

Father, You have said that You will never leave me or forsake me. Therefore, I can say without any doubt or fear that You are my Helper, and I am not afraid of anything that mere man can do to me. You are greater in me than he who is in the world. If You are for me, who can be against me? I am free from the fear of man and the pressure of public opinion.

Father, You have not given me a spirit of timidity (of cowardice, of craven and cringing and fawning fear), but [You have given me a spirit of] power and of love and of a calm and well-balanced mind and discipline and self-control. I can do all things through Christ, Who gives me strength.

In Jesus' name I pray, amen.

Scripture References

1 John 1:9	2 Timothy 1:7 AMP
Hebrews 13:5,6	Ephesians 1:19,20
Genesis 1:27	Philippians 4:13 NIV
1 John 4:4	Colossians 1:29
Ephesians 2:10	Proverbs 29:25
Romans 8:31	Psalm 27:1
Luke 17:21	

Developing Perseverance

Father, the course that You have set before me is clear. You called me to start this business, and I look to You as my Partner in it. I purpose to be strong, courageous and firm.

Lord, thank You for going before me and working with me; You will not fail me or let me go or forsake me. In the name of Jesus, I resist cowardice and fear, refusing to become broken [in spirit] (depressed, dismayed and unnerved with alarm).

Through the power of the Holy Spirit I throw off those things that hinder me, and the sin that so easily entangles me, for I desire to run with perseverance the race marked out for me. I fix my eyes on Jesus, the author and perfecter of my faith, Who for the joy set before Him endured the cross, scorning its shame, and sat down at the right hand of Your throne. I consider Him Who endured such opposition from sinful men, so that I will not grow weary and lose heart and give up in times of stress (employee turnover, decreased cash flow, rising costs, etc.).

By the grace wherein I stand, I trust in and rely on You, my Lord; my hope and confidence are in You. On the authority of Your Word I declare and decree that I am like a tree planted by the waters that spreads out its roots by the river; I shall not see and fear when heat comes, but my leaf shall be green; I shall not be anxious and careful in the year of drought, nor shall I cease from yielding fruit.

I pray that your Holy Spirit will bring this commitment to my remembrance when I grow weary and overburdened with the responsibilities of this company.

In every prayer of mine I always make entreaty and petition with joy [delight] for my associates and employees. I am convinced and sure of this very thing: that He Who began a good work in this company will continue until the day of Jesus Christ—developing and perfecting and bringing it to full completion.

Thank You for creating in me a steadfast, joyous spirit. I rejoice and exult in hope, remaining steadfast and patient in trouble, for You, Father, are my exceeding joy.

In Jesus' name I pray, amen.

Scripture References

Deuteronomy 31:6-8 AMP

Psalm 51:10 AMP

Hebrews 12:1-3 NIV

Romans 12:12 AMP

Jeremiah 17:7,8 AMP

Psalm 43:4

Philippians 1:4,6 AMP

Controlling Conversation by Wisdom

DEVOTIONAL READING

If you are wise, live a life of steady goodness, so that only good deeds will pour forth.
And if you don't brag about them, then you will
be truly wise! And by all means don't brag
about being wise and good if you are bitter and
jealous and selfish; that is the worst sort of lie.
For jealousy and selfishness are not God's kind
of wisdom. Such things are earthly, unspiritual,
inspired by the devil. For wherever there is jealousy or selfish ambition, there will be disorder
and every kind of evil.

But the wisdom that comes from heaven is
first of all pure and full of quiet gentleness.
Then it is peace-loving and courteous. It
allows discussion and is willing to yield to
others; it is full of mercy and good deeds. It is
wholehearted and straightforward and sincere.

And those who are peacemakers will plant
seeds of peace and reap a harvest of goodness.

James 3:13-18 TLB

MEDITATION

One of the greatest hindrances to forming healthy working relationships is a lack of open, honest communication. Impure motives will cause us to use words of flattery to control others or deceitful words to conceal greedy motives or as pretexts for selfish gain.

Often we demand to be understood rather than seeking to understand. Too many times our conversation is controlled by envy, selfishness, jealousy and personal ambition. The writer of the book of James calls this self-indulgent orientation earthly, unspiritual wisdom, and says that it is inspired by the devil.

Let us overcome our enslaving fears, agitating passions and moral conflicts and determine to become peacemakers. We sow seeds of peace by speaking words of peace from a pure heart. Then we will reap a harvest of goodness in our business dealings as well as in our private lives.

PRAYER

Father, I desire that my conversation and my behavior be controlled by the wisdom that comes from heaven, which is first of all pure. I believe in goodness, and I value Your approval; therefore, I fix my mind on whatever is true and honorable and just and pure and lovely and admirable. I model my conduct on what I have learned from the Scriptures, and the God of peace is with me.

I purify my soul in obeying the truth through the Spirit in sincere love for my fellow workers, whom I love fervently with a pure heart.

It is my prayer that I will overflow more and more with love for others, while at the same time growing in spiritual knowledge and insight, for I want always to see clearly the difference between right and wrong and to be inwardly clean. May I always be doing those good, kind things that show I am a child of God, for this will bring much praise and glory to You.

Father, I submit to Your Word, which is living and active. Sharper than any two-edged sword; it penetrates even to dividing soul and spirit, joints and marrow; it judges the thoughts and attitudes of my heart.

Surely You desire truth in the inner parts; You teach me wisdom in the inmost place. Cleanse me with hyssop, and I will be clean; wash me, and I will be whiter than snow.

In Jesus' name I pray, amen.

Scripture References

Philippians 4:8,9 PHILLIPS

Psalm 51:6,7 NIV

Hebrews 4:12 NIV

Philippians 1:9-11 TLB

1 Peter 1:22 NKJV

Manifesting Gentleness

Father, I desire to be a leader controlled by Your wisdom, which is full of quiet gentleness. Reveal to me by Your Spirit how to be equitable, fair, moderate and forbearing in dealing with my associates. I desire to look at situations humanely and reasonably rather than insisting on the letter of the law.

In the name of Jesus, I will not be combative but gentle and kind and considerate, not quarrelsome but forbearing and peaceable, and not a lover of money. I seek to be submissive, obedient, prepared and willing to do any upright and honorable work.

I will not slander or abuse or speak evil of anyone (my associates, customers, friends, family members or competitors). I avoid contentiousness. In the name of Jesus, I am forbearing (yielding, gentle and conciliatory), and I affirm that I will show unqualified courtesy toward everybody.

Father, I desire that my administration of this organization not be burdensome or irksome to others. I purpose to be gentle among my employees and staff. When necessary, help me to be like a mother caring for her little children.

I recognize that "gentleness is love in action—being considerate, meeting the needs of others, allowing time for the other person to talk and being willing to learn." Help me maintain a gentle attitude in my relationships with others.

In Jesus' name I pray, amen.

Scripture References

James 3:17 TLB   1 Timothy 3:3

Titus 3:1-3 AMP   1 Thessalonians 2:7 NIV

Showing Mercy

Father, in the name of Jesus, I am Your child and an imitator of You. You are so rich in mercy that You gave me back my life even though I was spiritually dead and doomed by my sins. It was by Your undeserved favor towards me that I was redeemed and set free. At Your invitation, I pray boldly for mercy for myself and for my associates, competitors, family and friends.

As Your chosen child, holy and dearly loved, I clothe myself with compassion, kindness, humility, gentleness and patience. I bear with others and forgive whatever grievances I may have against them. I forgive as You, Lord, forgave me. And over all these virtues I put on love, which binds them all together in perfect unity.

Help me to make allowances for another's faults, realizing that through gentleness and humility I might help him back onto the right path, while remembering that the next time I may be the one in the wrong.

Help me and my co-workers to share each other's trouble and problems appropriately. Let us be sure that we are doing our very best, for then we will have the personal satisfaction of work well done and won't need to compare ourselves with someone else. Each of us must bear some faults and burdens of his own, for none of us is perfect!

Father, I renounce self-righteousness and pride that would cause me to despise others and cut me off from Your mercy. Jesus said that if I am merciful to others, I will be shown mercy. Therefore I choose to manifest mercy.

In Jesus' name I pray, amen.

Scripture References

Ephesians 5:1 NIV

Galatians 6:1-5 TLB

Colossians 3:12-14 NIV

Hebrews 4:16

Ephesians 2:4 TLB

Matthew 5:7 NIV

Overcoming a Business Failure

DEVOTIONAL READING

May the Lord answer [me] when [I am]
    in distress;
      may the name of the God of Jacob
        protect [me].

May he send [me] help from the sanctuary
    and grant [me] support from Zion.

May he remember all [my] sacrifices
    and accept [my] burnt offerings.

May he give [me] the desire of [my] heart
    and make all [my] plans succeed.

[I] will shout for joy when [I am] victorious
and will lift up [my banner] in the
      name of [my] God.

May the Lord grant all [my] requests.

Now I know that the Lord saves his anointed;
    he answers him from his holy heaven
    with the saving power of his right hand

Some trust in chariots and some in horses,
but [I] trust in the name of the
Lord [my] God.

They are brought to their knees and fall,
but [I] rise up and stand firm.

Lord, save the king!
Answer [me] when [I] call!

Psalm 20:1-9 NIV

MEDITATION

The writer of Psalm 20 lived under the old covenant. Today we are living in the age of a new covenant and do not offer up sacrifices of animals. Instead, Jesus, the Lamb of God, gave Himself to be crucified on the cross of Calvary as the perfect sacrifice for our sins and for the sins of the whole world. In so doing, He provided for us everything we need in this life and the next:

The high priest carries the blood of animals
into the Most Holy Place as a sin offering, but

the bodies are burned outside the camp. And so Jesus also suffered outside the city gate to make the people holy through his own blood. Let us, then, go to him outside the camp, bearing the disgrace he bore. For here we do not have an enduring city, but we are looking for the city that is to come.

Through Jesus, therefore, let us continually offer to God a sacrifice of praise—the fruit of lips that confess his name. And do not forget to do good and to share with others, for with such sacrifices God is pleased.

Hebrews 13:11-16 NIV

PRAYER

Father, You see my disappointment and distress over this business setback. I poured many hours of study and preparation into this deal. My plans were carefully laid. I believed and expected it to prosper, but now it seems that all of my work was in vain.

I look to You, O Lord. Help me to learn of You, even in the midst of this adversity, and to remain strong in You and in Your mighty power.

Father, I believe that You brought me to this position I hold today, and I will not be afraid, for You turn into good what is intended for my undoing.

You are God, and there is no other; there is none like You. You know the end from the beginning—from ancient times, what is still to come. Your purpose in this situation shall stand, and You will do all that You please.

I refuse to be amazed and bewildered at the fiery ordeal which is taking place to test my quality, as though something strange (unusual and alien to me and my position) were befalling me.

Father, I remember that Your blessing brings wealth, and You add no trouble to it. There is surely a future hope for me, and my hope will not be cut off. I have sown, that good might come to others; and I believe that I shall reap in due season, if I faint not.

…O my soul, don't be discouraged. Don't be upset. Expect God to act! For I know that I shall again have plenty of reason to praise him for all that he will do. He is my help! He is my God! (Ps. 42:11 TLB).

Lord, I offer up to You sacrifices of praise—the fruit of my lips, which confess Your name—and I will not forget to do good and to share with others, for with such sacrifices You are pleased.

In Jesus' name I pray, amen.

Scripture References

Ephesians 6:10 NIV	Isaiah 46:8-10 NIV
Proverbs 10:22 NIV	Galatians 6:9
Genesis 50:20 TLB	1 Peter 4:12 AMP
Proverbs 23:18 NIV	Hebrews 13:15,16 NIV

Deliverance from Habits

Father, in the name of Jesus and according to Your Word, I believe in my heart and say with my mouth that Jesus is Lord of my life. Since all truth is in Jesus, I strip myself of my former nature [put off and discard my old, unrenewed self]. I desire to be free from the habit(s) of _____, in the name of Jesus. Father, this/these habit(s) is/are not helpful (good for me, expedient and profitable when considered with other things). I no longer desire to be the slave of wrong habits and behaviors or be brought under their power.

Father, these self-destructive habits are symptoms of a flaw in my soul, my character, and I confess them as sin. I don't want to habitually make the same mistakes over and over. Father, Your Word exposes the wrong thought patterns that are driving me to continue acting out in ways that are contrary to Your Word. I desire to be continually filled with and controlled by the Holy Spirit.

Thank You, Father, for translating me into the Kingdom of Your dear Son. Now I am Your garden under cultivation. In the name of Jesus, I throw all spoiled virtue and cancerous evil in the garbage. In simple humility, I purpose to let You, my gardener, landscape me with the Word, making a salvation-garden of my life.

I arm myself with the full armor of God, that armor of a heavily armed soldier which God has supplied for me—the helmet of salvation, loins girded with truth, feet shod with the preparation of the gospel of peace, the shield of faith, and the sword of the Spirit, which is the Word of God. With God's armor on, I am able to stand up against all the strategies and deceits and fiery darts of Satan, in the name of Jesus.

Clothed in Your armor, I discipline my body and subdue it. With every temptation, I choose the way of escape that You provide. Greater is He that is in me than he that is in the world.

Thank You, Lord. I praise You that I am growing spiritually, and Your engrafted Word is saving my soul. I strip away the old nature with its habits, and I put on the new man created in Christ Jesus. Hallelujah! Amen.

Scripture References

Romans 10:9,10

Ephesians 4:21,22

1 Corinthians 6:12 AMP

1 Corinthians 3:9 AMP

James 1:21 MESSAGE

1 Corinthians 10:13

1 John 4:4

A Company, Office or Department

Father, in the name of Jesus, I desire that the work of our hands, our labor in the _____ department/office here at _____ be productive for Your glory and for the good and profit of all. You have given us everything we need to live a full and useful life.

We are individuals who are [mutually dependent on one another], having gifts that differ according to the grace given us. We, who with unveiled faces all reflect Your glory, are being transformed into Your likeness with ever-increasing glory, which comes from You, Who are the Spirit.

Father, I realize that You know what we have need of before we ask, and that we are not all growing in the same manner or on the same time schedule, but we are growing in the grace and knowledge of our Lord and Savior, Jesus Christ.

We give each other space to grow, for we are becoming a patient people, bearing with one another. We acknowledge that we do not have dominion [over] each other, and we refuse to lord it over one another's faith, but we are fellow laborers to promote one another's joy, because it is by faith that we stand strong.

In Jesus' name I pray, amen.

Scripture References

2 Peter 1:3,4

2 Peter 3:18

Romans 12:5,6 AMP

2 Corinthians 1:24 AMP

2 Corinthians 3:18 NIV

Ephesians 4:2 AMP

Matthew 6:32

A Person in Need of Salvation

Father, in the name of Jesus, I make a joyful noise to the Lord, and serve You with gladness! I come before You with singing! I know that You are God!

It is written in Your Word that Jesus came to seek and save the lost. You wish all people to be saved and to know Your divine truth. Therefore, Father, I bring _____ before You this day.

Thank You for calling me to be Your agent of intercession for _____. By the grace of God I will build up the wall and stand in the gap before You for _____, that he/she might be spared from eternal destruction.

Father, thank You for salvation. I acknowledge Jesus as the Lamb of God, Who takes away _____'s sins, and the Holy Spirit, Who convicts and convinces him/her of sin, righteousness and judgment. Your kindness leads _____ to repent (to change his/her mind and inner man to accept Your will). You are the One Who delivers _____ and draws him/her to Yourself out of the control and the dominion of darkness and transfers him/her into the Kingdom of the Son of Your love.

Father, I pray that _____ will hear the truth from someone standing in Your presence. The Good News was hidden from _____. Satan, the god of this world, made him/her blind, and he/she was unable to see the glorious light of the gospel. Now, I ask You, Lord of the harvest, to thrust the perfect laborer into _____'s path to share Your gospel in a special way so that he/she will listen and understand it. As Your laborer ministers to him/her, I believe that he/she will come to his/her senses—come out of the snare of the devil who has held him/her captive—and make Jesus the Lord of his/her life.

Having prayed all that I know to pray, I submit to the Spirit, Who also helps me in my present limitations. I do not always know how to pray worthily, but Your Spirit within me is actually praying for me in those agonizing longings which cannot find words. Having done all to stand, I stand on Your Word, and Father, I shall praise You and thank You for _____'s salvation. I commit this matter into Your hands, and with my faith I see _____ saved and filled with Your Spirit, with a full and clear knowledge of Your Word.

Amen—so be it!*

Scripture References

Psalm 100:1-3 AMP

Colossians 1:13 AMP

Luke 19:10

2 Corinthians 4:2-4 TLB

2 Peter 3:9

Matthew 9:38 AMP

Ezekiel 22:30 AMP

2 Timothy 2:26 NIV

John 1:29

Romans 8:26 PHILLIPS

John 16:8-12 AMP

Ephesians 6:13

Romans 2:4 AMP

NOTE TO READER

When you are praying for an individual's salvation, it is necessary that you allow patience to have her perfect work. Stand against discouragement, doubt and unbelief by enforcing the victory Jesus won at Calvary. The Lord is your confidence, and your prayer must be founded on the faithfulness of God. Ask forgiveness when you are doubtful or distrustful, and continue fighting the "good fight of faith."

In your intercession you will be up against a stronghold of independence, which separates mankind from God. Inappropriate independence reinforces self-conceit: "No one will tell me what to do."

Those who are lost cannot discern the truth. If the eyes of their heart are to be flooded with light so that they can know and understand truth, the veil of pride must be removed.

Satan cannot control the mind of the unbeliever, but he does influence his/her thinking. Your prayers initiate mind-liberation when you engage God's mighty weapons to knock down the devil's strongholds—proud arguments against God. You can knock down walls that keep men from finding Him. (Read 2 Corinthians 4 and Ephesians 1:18)

Maintain your prayer armor and wield the sword of the Spirit, which is the Word of God (Eph. 6:10-18).

Proclaim aloud: With God's mighty weapons I can capture _____ and bring him/her back to God and influence _____ into being a man/woman whose heart's desire is obedience to Christ. (2 Cor. 10:3-6 TLB) I will not give up but I will pray until _____ receives a revelation—the lifting of the veil.

Praise: I rejoice because the counsel of hell shall not prevail against _____'s salvation. Thank you, Father, that the illuminating light of the knowledge of the glory of God is revealed to _____. You are bringing him/her to repentance by your goodness, and he/she will receive a new knowledge that will replace his/her arrogant thinking. Amen

Satan, you have no choice. _____ is protected by the blood of Jesus. _____ is no longer under your authority. Now _____ belongs to Jesus!

* *After you have prayed this prayer, thank the Lord for this person's salvation. Rejoice and praise God for the victory! Confess the above prayer as done! Thank the Lord for sending the laborer. Thank Him that Satan is defeated. Hallelujah!*

A Person in Need of Protection

Father, in the name of Jesus, I lift up _____
to you and pray a hedge of protection around him/her.
I thank You, Father, that You are a wall of fire around
about _____ and that You have sent Your angels
to encamp around about him/her.

I thank You, Father, that _____ dwells in
the secret place of the Most High and abides under
the shadow of the Almighty. I say of You, Lord, that
You are his/her refuge and fortress: his/her God; in
You will he/she trust. You cover _____ with
Your feathers, and under Your wings shall he/she trust.
Your truth shall be his/her shield and buckler.

_____ shall not be afraid of the terror by
night, nor of the arrow that flies by day. Only with
his/her eyes will he/she behold and see the reward of
the wicked.

Because _____ has made You, Lord,
his/her refuge and habitation, no evil shall befall

him/her—no accident will overtake him/her—neither shall any plague or calamity come near him/her. For You will give Your angels charge over him/her, to keep him/her in all Your ways.

Father, because _____ has set his/her love upon You, therefore will You deliver him/her. He/she shall call upon You, and You will answer him/her.

You will be with _____ in trouble; You will deliver him/her and will satisfy him/her with long life and show him/her Your salvation.

In Jesus' name I pray, amen.

Scripture References

Job 1:10
Zechariah 2:5
Psalm 34:7
Psalm 91:1,2

Psalm 91:4,5
Psalm 91:8-11
Psalm 91:14-16

Person in Need of Employment

Father, in Jesus' name, I believe and confess Your Word over _____ today, knowing that you watch over Your Word to perform it. Your Word prospers in _____, to whom it is sent!

Father, You are _____'s source of every comfort (consolation and encouragement). He/she is courageous and grows in strength.

_____'s desire is to owe no man anything except to love him. Therefore, he/she is strong and lets not his/her hands be weak and slack, for his/her work shall be rewarded. His/her wages are not counted as a favor or a gift, but as an obligation (something owed to him/her).

_____ makes it his/her ambition and definitely endeavors to live quietly and peacefully, to mind his/her own affairs and to work with his/her hands. He/she is correct and honorable and commands the respect of the outside world, being dependent on nobody [self-supporting], and having need of nothing, for You, Father, supply (fill to the full) his/her every need.

_____ works in quietness and earns his/her own food and other necessities. He/she is not weary of doing right [but continues in well-doing without weakening]. He/she learns to apply himself/herself to good deeds (to honest labor and honorable employ-ment) so that he/she is able to meet necessary demands whenever the occasion may require.

Father, You know [the record of] _____'s works and what he/she is doing. You have set before him/her a door wide open, which no one is able to shut.

_____ does not fear and is not dismayed, for you, Father, strengthen him/her. You help him/her, in Jesus' name. In Jesus _____ has [perfect] peace and confidence and is of good cheer, because Jesus overcame the world and deprived it of its power to harm _____.

_____ does not fret or have anxiety about anything, for Your peace, Father, mounts guard over his/her heart and mind.

_____ knows the secret of facing every situation, [for he/she is self-sufficient in Christ's sufficiency]. He/she guards his/her mouth and his/her tongue, keeping himself/herself from trouble.

_____ prizes Your wisdom, Father, and acknowledges You. You direct and make straight and plain his/her path, and You promote him/her.

Therefore, Father, _____ increases in Your wisdom (in broad and full understanding) and in stature and years, and in favor with You and man!

In Jesus' name I pray, amen.

Scripture References

Jeremiah 1:12 AMP

Isaiah 55:11 AMP

2 Corinthians 1:3 AMP

1 Corinthians 16:13 AMP

Romans 13:8 AMP

2 Chronicles 15:7 AMP

Romans 4:4 AMP

1 Thessalonians 4:11,12 AMP

Philippians 4:19 AMP

2 Thessalonians 3:12,13 AMP

Titus 3:14 AMP

Revelation 3:8 AMP

Isaiah 41:10 AMP

John 16:33 AMP

Philippians 4:6,7 AMP

Philippians 4:12,13 AMP

Proverbs 21:23 AMP

Proverbs 3:6 AMP

Proverbs 4:8 AMP

Luke 2:52 AMP

A Person Experiencing Grief or Loss

Father, in the name of Jesus, I approach Your throne of grace, bringing _____ before You. I recognize that grieving is a human emotional process, and I give him/her the space that he/she needs to enter into the rest that You have for him/her.

Lord, Jesus bore _____'s griefs (sicknesses, weaknesses and distresses) and carried his/her sorrows and pains; I know that Your Spirit is upon Jesus to bind up and heal _____'s broken heart. May he/she be gentle with himself/herself, knowing that he/she is not alone in his/her grief. You are with him/her, and You will never leave him/her without support.

Father, I desire to be a doer of Your Word, and not a hearer only. Therefore, I make a commitment to rejoice with those who rejoice [sharing others' joy], and to weep with those who weep [sharing others' grief]. I pray that my love will give _____ great joy and comfort and encouragement, because he/she has refreshed the hearts of Your people.

Thank You, Father, for sending the Holy Spirit to comfort, counsel, help, intercede for, defend, strengthen and stand by _____ in this time of grief and sorrow.

In Jesus' name I pray, amen.

Scripture References

Isaiah 53:4 AMP

Isaiah 61:1 AMP

Hebrews 13:5 AMP

2 Corinthians 12:9 PHILLIPS

Galatians 6:2 PHILLIPS

Ephesians 4:2 AMP

James 1:22

Romans 12:15 AMP

Galatians 6:2 AMP

Philemon 7 AMP

John 14:26

Home and Family

Father, I thank You that You have blessed me and my family with all spiritual blessings in Christ Jesus.

Through skillful and godly wisdom is my house (my life, my home, my family) built, and by understanding it is established [on a sound and good foundation]. And by knowledge shall its chambers [of every area] be filled with all precious and pleasant riches—great [priceless] treasure. The house of the [uncompromisingly] righteous shall stand. Prosperity and welfare are in my house, in the name of Jesus.

My house is securely built. It is founded on a rock—revelation knowledge of Your Word, Father. Jesus is its Cornerstone. Jesus is Lord of my household. Jesus is our Lord—spirit, soul and body.

Whatever may be our task, we work at it heartily (from the soul), as [something done] for You, Lord, and not for men. We love each other with the God-kind of love, and we dwell in peace. Our home is

PRAYERS THAT AVAIL MUCH FOR THE WORKPLACE

committed to You [deposited into Your charge, entrusted to Your protection and care].

Father, I know not what others may do, but as for me and my house, we will serve the Lord! Hallelujah!

In Jesus' name I pray, amen.

Scripture References

Ephesians 1:3	Acts 16:31 AMP
Proverbs 24:3,4 AMP	Philippians 2:10,11 AMP
Proverbs 15:6 AMP	Colossians 3:23 AMP
Proverbs 12:7	Colossians 3:14,15 NIV
Psalm 112:3 AMP	Acts 20:32 AMP
Luke 6:48 AMP	Joshua 24:15
Acts 4:11 AMP	

Children at School

Father, I confess Your Word this day concerning my children as they pursue their education and training at school. You are effectually at work in them [energizing and creating in them the power and desire] both to will and to work for Your good pleasure. They are the head and not the tail, above only and not beneath.

I pray that my children will find favor, good understanding and high esteem in sight [or judgment] of You and man—their teachers and classmates.

I ask You to give my children wisdom and understanding as knowledge is presented to them in all fields of study and endeavor.

Father, thank You for giving them the aptitude for every kind of learning, that they may be well informed, quick to understand and qualified to serve You. I ask

You to help us (the parents and our children) remember that the fear of the Lord is the beginning of knowledge.

Thank You that my children have the appetite of the diligent; they are abundantly supplied with educational resources and their thoughts are those of the steadily diligent, which tend only to achievement. Thank You that they are growing in wisdom and knowledge.

I will not cease to pray for my children, asking that they be filled with the knowledge of Your will, bearing fruit in every good work.

Father, I thank You that my children have divine protection since they dwell in the secret place of the Most High. They trust and find their refuge in You and stand rooted and grounded in Your love. They shall not be led astray by philosophies of men and teaching that is contrary to truth. You are their shield and buckler, protecting them from all attacks or threats. Thank You for the angels whom You have assigned to them to accompany and defend and preserve them in all their ways [of obedience and service]. My children are established in Your love, which turns all fear out of doors and expels every trace of terror.

I pray that the teachers of my children will be godly men and women of integrity. Give them understanding hearts and wisdom in order that they may walk in the ways of piety and virtue, revering Your holy name.

In Jesus' name I pray, amen.

Scripture References

Philippians 2:13 AMP

Deuteronomy 28:1,2,13 AMP

Proverbs 3:4 AMP

1 Kings 4:29

Daniel 1:4 NIV

Proverbs 1:7 NIV

Colossians 1:9,10 NIV

Psalm 91:1,2 AMP

Ephesians 3:17

Ephesians 4:14

Psalm 91:3-11 AMP

1 John 4:18 AMP

Proverbs 21:5 RSV, TLB, AMP

An Employer's Personal Prayer

Father, in the name of Jesus, I resolve to be as conscientious and responsible toward those who work for me as I expect them to be toward me. I will not misuse the power over others that has been placed in my hands, and I will not forget that I am responsible myself to a heavenly Supervisor Who makes no distinction between employer and employee.

As an employer I realize that my responsibility is to be just and fair toward those I employ. I purpose always to maintain the habit of prayer for them: to be alert and thankful as I pray for each person to find favor with You and with man. Help me always to give honor where honor is due.

Give me Your discernment for those with whom I labor, that I might see their hidden potential and draw it out, helping them to become all that You created them to be.

I value my employees as persons called of You for their appointed tasks. I thank You for their abilities and talents, and I ask You to make me sensitive to their spiritual and emotional needs. Although I could be bold and order my associates to do what they ought to do, help me to appeal to them always on the basis of Your love.

Thank You for Your power and ability, which enable me to do unto them as I would have them do unto me. Help me to follow Jesus as my example in all that I say and do.

In His name I pray, amen.

Scripture References

Ephesians 6:9 PHILLIPS

Colossians 4:1,2 PHILLIPS

Luke 2:52

Romans 13:7

Philemon 8,9 NIV

Matthew 7:12 NIV

1 Peter 2:21 NIV

Establishing Communication With Co-workers

Father, to as many as received Jesus, You gave the power to become Your sons and daughters. I am learning to be straightforward in my communication with my brothers and sisters in Christ, my co-laborers in the Lord. I have the power to be direct, honestly expressing my feelings and desires, because Jesus has been made unto me wisdom. Wisdom from above is straightforward, impartial (unbiased, objective) and unfeigned (free from doubts, wavering and insincerity).

I am Your creation, Father, and You created me to be active in sharing my faith, so that I will have a full understanding of every good thing we have in Christ. It is my prayer that my conversation will always be full of grace, seasoned with salt, so that I may know how to answer everyone. I am content with my own reality (satisfied to the point where I am not disturbed or disquieted) in whatever state I am, so those around me can feel safe in my presence. I will speak truly, deal truly and live truly, expressing the truth in love.

As Your children and co-laborers, we walk in the ever-developing maturity that enables us to be in perfect harmony and full agreement in what we say, perfectly united in our common understanding and in our opinions and judgments. And if on some point we think differently, You will make it clear to us. We live up to what we have already attained in our individual lives and in our group. We will let our yes be simply yes, and our no be simply no.

In Jesus' name I pray, amen.

Scripture References

John 1:12	Philippians 4:11 AMP
1 Corinthians 1:30	Ephesians 4:15 AMP
James 3:17 AMP	1 Corinthians 1:10 AMP
Philemon 6 NIV	Philippians 3:15-17 NIV
Colossians 4:6 NIV	Matthew 5:37 AMP

Forgiving Others

Clothed in Your armor, Father, I forgive anyone who has caused me distress, grief, embarrassment and/or financial loss. I choose to forgive in the sight of Christ, in order that Satan might not outwit me. For I am aware of his schemes.

Father, in the name of Jesus, I subject myself to You and resist the devil [stand firm against him], and he will flee from me. I let go of all bitterness and indignation and wrath (passion, rage, bad temper) and resentment (anger, animosity) and quarreling (brawling, clamor, contention) and slander (evil-speaking, abusive or blasphemous language). I am ready to be useful and helpful and kind to others, tenderhearted (compassionate, understanding, loving-hearted), forgiving others [readily and freely], as You in Christ forgave me.

I accept life and make a commitment to be patient and tolerant with others, always ready to forgive if I

have a difference with anyone. I forgive as freely as
You have forgiven me. And, above everything else, I
am truly loving, for love binds all the virtues together
in perfection.

In Jesus' name, amen.

Scripture References

Ephesians 6:11

2 Corinthians 2:5-11 NIV

James 4:7 AMP

Ephesians 4:31,32 AMP

Colossians 3:12-14

    PHILLIPS

Improving Harmony and Cooperation

DEVOTIONAL READING

Fill up and complete my joy by living in harmony and being of the same mind and one in purpose, having the same love, being in full accord and of one harmonious mind and intention.

Philippians 2:2 AMP

PRAYER

Father, Jesus prayed that His followers would be one. I enter into agreement with my Lord, praying for the development of harmony and cooperation among the leadership and employees of _____ *(company name)*. I ask for wisdom to know how to resolve any conflicts that may have arisen among the departments.

As _____ *(president, supervisor, manager, etc.)* of _____ I institute the principles of peace, uprooting and dissolving confusion, rivalries, arguments,

and disagreements for the good of our company,
_____, and the welfare of all concerned.

In the name of Jesus I submit myself to You,
Father, and resist the devil. I overcome the fear of
confrontation (and its outcome) and initiate resolution.
I desire to pursue peace with my co-workers,
customers, family and friends.

Give me the courage to go to anyone who is
holding anything against me, that we might be reconciled. Then I will come and offer my gift to You.

Also, I ask for the boldness of the Lion of Judah
to go to anyone who has sinned against me and
_____ *(company name)*, confronting his/her
fault without attacking him/her. I am requesting and
believing for reconciliation. Help me to forgive, even if
he/she refuses to be reconciled, and follow through
with the necessary steps for his/her good and the
company's welfare.

Thank You for the harmony and cooperation
necessary to accomplish our common goals.

Glory be to You Who, by Your mighty power at work within us, are able to do far more than we would ever dare to ask or even dream of—infinitely beyond our highest prayers, desires, thoughts or hopes. May You be given glory for ever and ever through endless ages because of Your master plan of salvation for the Church through Jesus Christ.

In Jesus' name I pray, amen.

Scripture References

John 17:21   Matthew 5:23,24

James 1:5   Matthew 18:15

James 4:7   Ephesians 3:20,21 TLB

Hebrews 12:14 NKJV

Making Decisions on the Basis of Love

DEVOTIONAL READING

And let the peace (soul harmony which comes) from Christ rule (act as umpire continually) in your hearts [deciding and settling with finality all questions that arise in your minds, in that peaceful state] to which as [members of Christ's] one body you were also called [to live]. And be thankful (appreciative), [giving praise to God always].

Colossians 3:15 AMP

MEDITATION

Whether your business decisions are made by you alone or by a board of trustees, pray the following for assurance and confidence. Pray the same prayer also for those to whom you have delegated the authority to make decisions, entrusting them to God, Who directs their steps. Sometimes mistakes will be made, but the Lord is bigger than our mistakes.

PRAYER

Father, I realize that before I can love others as You have instructed me, I must love myself. Help me to speak truly, deal truly and live truly in harmony with You, myself and others. I am Your workmanship, re-created in Christ Jesus, that I may do those good works which You, Lord, predestined (planned beforehand) for me [taking paths which You prepared ahead of time], that I should walk in them [living the good life which You prearranged and made ready for me to live].

According to Your Word, I am fearfully and wonderfully made. Help me to remember that although others do not always know what is best for me or this business to which You have called me, there is safety in a multitude of counselors, and so I weigh and consider their advice before taking action. I accept my responsibility as a leader (owner, employer, supervisor, manager, chairman of the board) to make the final decision concerning company issues, business transactions and corporate policies. I trust in You with all my heart and lean not on my own understanding; in all my ways I acknowledge You, and You direct my paths. I look to You to cause my thoughts to be agreeable to Your will, that I might make wise and healthy choices.

Give me the courage to make decisions that are in agreement with Your purpose and plan for my life and the lives of my associates. My yes shall be yes—my no, no.

Strengthened with Your power and might, I do nothing from factional motives [through contentiousness, strife, selfishness or for unworthy ends] or prompted by conceit and empty arrogance. I am not [merely] concerned with my own interests, but also with the interests of others. I desire to do unto others as I would have them do unto me. I am walking uprightly before You; therefore, I consider, direct and establish my way [with the confidence of integrity].

You are my confidence, and You keep my foot from being snared. Your love is shed abroad in my heart. I love my neighbors—my fellow workers—as myself, and make decisions with their welfare in mind.

In Jesus' name I pray, amen.

Scripture References

Romans 13:9 AMP

Ephesians 4:15 AMP

Ephesians 2:10 AMP

Psalm 139:14

Proverbs 11:14

Proverbs 3:5,6

Proverbs 16:3 AMP

Romans 8:28 NIV

Matthew 5:37 AMP

Colossians 1:11

Philippians 2:3,4 AMP

Matthew 7:12 AMP

Proverbs 21:29 AMP

Proverbs 3:26 NIV

Romans 5:5

Luke 10:27

Overcoming Negative Work Attitudes

Lord Jesus, You are my High Priest with ready access to God, and you are not out of touch with reality. You have been through weakness and testing, experienced it all—all but the sin. So I have come to receive mercy and accept the help that you are so ready to give.

I acknowledge my sin of rebellion, and ask forgiveness for my negative attitude toward my employer, boss and co-workers. I admit my sins— make a clean breast of them—and You won't let me down; You'll be true to Yourself. Thank You for forgiving my sins and purging me of all wrongdoing. I am an overcomer by the blood of the Lamb and the word of my testimony.

In the name of Jesus, I pull down the strongholds of distrust and suspicion that have protected and rein-forced my rebellious thought patterns, wrong motives, wrong attitudes and bad feelings toward others. I bind my mind to the mind of Christ, and my will to the will of God. I loose myself from self-centered and selfish thinking.

I submit to the constant ministry of transformation by the Holy Spirit, and take my everyday, ordinary life—my sleeping, eating, going-to-work, and walking-around life—and place it before You, my God, as an offering. I fix my attention on You, and I will be changed from the inside out.

Father, I choose to be obedient to my employers and respect them, and I am eager to please them in singleness of motive and with all my heart as [service] to Christ, not in the way of eye-service [as if they were watching me] but as a servant of Christ, doing Your will heartily and with my whole soul.

I will render service with goodwill, as to You and not to men. I know that for whatever good I do, I will receive my reward from You.

Father, I ask You to help me do everything readily and cheerfully—without bickering and second-guessing. I purpose to go out into the world uncorrupted, a breath of fresh air in the squalid and polluted society. May I provide people with a glimpse of good living and of the living God.

I revere You, Lord, and my work is a sincere expression of my devotion to You. Whatever may be my task, I work at it heartily (from the soul), as something done for You, knowing that the One I am actually serving is the Lord Christ (the Messiah). In His name I pray, amen.

Scripture References

Hebrews 4:14-16 MESSAGE

1 John 1:9 MESSAGE

Revelation 12:11

2 Corinthians 10:5

Matthew 18:18

2 Corinthians 3:18

Romans 12:1,2 MESSAGE

Ephesians 6:5-8 AMP

Philippians 1:14,15 MESSAGE

Colossians 3:22-24 AMP

Part V

Prayers for Guidance and Attitude

To Seek Wisdom

DEVOTIONAL READING

My son, if you accept my words
>   and store up my commands within you,

turning your ear to wisdom
>   and applying your heart to understanding,

and if you call out for insight
>   and cry aloud for understanding,

and if you look for it as silver
>   and search for it as for hidden treasure,

then you will understand the fear of the Lord
>   and find the knowledge of God.

For the Lord gives wisdom,
>   and from his mouth come
>   knowledge and understanding.

He holds victory in store for the upright,
>   he is a shield to those whose walk is
>   blameless,

for he guards the course of the just
    and protects the way of his faithful ones.

Then you will understand what is right and just
    and fair—every good path.

For wisdom will enter your heart,
    and knowledge will be pleasant to your soul.

Discretion will protect you,
    and understanding will guard you.

Wisdom will save you from the ways
      of wicked men,
    from men whose words are perverse,

who leave the straight paths
    to walk in dark ways,

who delight in doing wrong
    and rejoice in the perverseness of evil,

whose paths are crooked
    and who are devious in their ways.

It will save you also from the adulteress,
    from the wayward wife with her
      seductive words,

who has left the partner of her youth
  and ignored the covenant she made
    before God.

For her house leads down to death
  and her paths to the spirits of the dead.

None who go to her return
  or attain the paths of life.

Thus you will walk in the ways of good men
  and keep to the paths of the righteous.

For the upright will live in the land,
  and the blameless will remain in it;

but the wicked will be cut off from the land,
  and the unfaithful will be torn from it.

Proverbs 2:1-22 NIV

PRAYER

Father, I thank you for filling me with Your Spirit, giving me great wisdom, ability and skill in accomplishing the work to which You have called me.

Thank You for imparting to me wisdom and understanding to know how to carry out all the work of establishing and building _____ *(name of firm)*. My mouth shall speak of wisdom, and the meditation of my heart shall be of understanding.

I thank You that I am in Christ Jesus, Who has become for me wisdom from You—that is, my righteousness, holiness and redemption. I am filled with the knowledge of Your will through all spiritual wisdom and understanding, that I may live a life worthy of You and may please You in every way: bearing fruit in every good work, growing in the knowledge of You.

In Jesus' name I pray, amen.

Scripture References

Exodus 31:3 TLB   Colossians 1:9,10 NIV
1 Corinthians 1:30 NIV   Psalm 49:3
Exodus 36:1

To Walk in God's Perfect Will

Lord and God, You are worthy to receive glory and honor and power, for You created all things; by Your will they were created and have their being. You adopted me as Your child through Jesus Christ, in accordance with Your pleasure and will. I pray that I may be active in sharing my faith, so that I will have a full understanding of every good thing I have in Christ.

Father, I ask You to give me a complete understanding of what You want to do in my life, and I ask You to make me wise with spiritual wisdom. Then the way I live will always honor and please You, and I will continually do good, kind things for others. All the while, I will learn to know You better and better.

Jesus has been made unto me wisdom. I single-mindedly walk in that wisdom, expecting to know what to do in every situation and to be on top of every circumstance!

I roll my works upon You [commit and trust them wholly to You: and You cause my thoughts to become agreeable to Your will, and] so my plans are established and succeed. You direct my steps and make them sure. I understand and firmly grasp what Your will is, for I am not vague, thoughtless and foolish. I stand firm and mature [in spiritual growth], convinced and fully assured in everything willed by You.

Father, You have destined and appointed me to come progressively to know Your will [to perceive, to recognize more strongly and clearly and to become better and more intimately acquainted with Your will].

I thank You, Father, for the Holy Spirit, Who abides [permanently] in me and guides me into all the truth (the whole, full truth) and speaks whatever He hears from You and announces and declares to me the things that are to come.

I have the mind of Christ and do hold the thoughts (feelings and purposes) of His heart.

So, Father, I have entered into Your blessed rest by believing (trusting in, clinging to and relying on) You.

Hallelujah!

In Jesus' name I pray, amen.

Scripture References

Philemon 6	James 1:5-8
Colossians 4:12 AMP	Hebrews 4:10 AMP
John 10:27	Proverbs 16:3,9 AMP
Acts 22:14 AMP	John 3:16 AMP
John 10:5	Ephesians 5:17 AMP
1 John 2:20,27 AMP	Proverbs 3:5,6
Colossians 1:9,10 AMP	Psalm 119:105
John 16:13 AMP	John 14:26
1 Corinthians 1:30	Joshua 1:8
1 Corinthians 2:16 AMP	James 1:22

To Trust in God

DEVOTIONAL READING

For all God's words are right, and everything
he does is worthy of our trust. He loves whatever
is just and good; the earth is filled with his tender
love. He merely spoke, and the heavens were
formed, and all the galaxies of stars. He made the
oceans, pouring them into his vast reservoirs.

Let everyone in all the world—men, women
and children—fear the Lord and stand in awe of
him. For when he but spoke, the world began! It
appeared at his command! And with a breath he
can scatter the plans of all the nations who oppose
him, but his own plan stands forever. His inten-
tions are the same for every generation.

Psalm 33:4-11 TLB

PRAYER

Father, I ask for grace to trust You more. When I
am afraid I will trust in You. I praise Your Word. My

God, in You I trust; I will not be afraid. What can mortal man do to me?

Lord, Your steadfast love never ceases, Your mercies never come to an end; they are new every morning; great is Your faithfulness. You are my portion; therefore, I will hope in You.

May You, the God of hope, fill me with all joy and peace as I trust in You, so that I may overflow with hope by the power of the Holy Spirit.

To You, O Lord, I pray and according to Your Word You will not fail me, for I am trusting You. None who has faith in You, Father, will ever be disgraced for trusting You.

Show me the path where I should go, O Lord; point out the right road for me to walk. Lead me; teach me; for You are the God Who gives me salvation.

Lord, I have no fear of bad news; my heart is steadfast, trusting in You. My heart is secure; I will have no fear.

Because You are faithful and trustworthy, I make a commitment to trust in You with all my heart and lean not on my own understanding; in all my ways I acknowledge You, and You will make my paths straight. I am blessed, for I trust in the Lord, in Whom is my confidence.

In Jesus' name I pray, amen.

Scripture References

Psalm 56:3,4 NIV   Romans 15:13 NIV

Psalm 112:7,8 NIV   Jeremiah 17:7 NIV

Lamentations 3:22-24 RSV   Psalm 25:1-5 TLB

Proverbs 3:5,6 NIV

To Use Discretion

DEVOTIONAL READING

Praise the Lord.
Blessed is the man who fears the Lord,
Who greatly delights in his commandments!
His descendants will be mighty in the land;
The generation of the upright will
be blessed.
Wealth and riches are in his house;
And his righteousness endures for ever.
Light rises in the darkness for the upright;
The Lord is gracious, merciful, and
righteous.
It is well with the man who deals generously
and lends,
who conducts his affairs with justice.
For the righteous will never be moved;
he will be remembered for ever.
He is not afraid of evil tidings;
his heart is firm, trusting in the Lord.
His heart is steady, he will not be afraid,
until he sees his desire on his adversaries.

He has distributed freely, he has given to the
poor;
his righteousness endures for ever;
his horn is exalted in honor.
The wicked man sees it and is angry;
he gnashes his teeth and melts away;
the desire of the wicked man comes to
nought.

Psalm 112:1-10 RSV

PRAYER

Father, I thank You for the virtue of discretion.

Lord, You give me knowledge and discretion.
Discretion protects me, and understanding guards me.

I preserve sound judgment and discernment; I will
not let them out of my sight; they will be life for me,
and an ornament to grace my neck. Then I will go on
my way in safety, and my foot will not stumble; when I
lie down, I will not be afraid; when I lie down, my
sleep will be sweet. I have no fear of sudden disaster or
of the ruin that overtakes the wicked, for You, Lord,

will be my confidence and will keep my foot from being snared.

Father, I pay attention to Your wisdom, and listen well to Your words of insight, that I may maintain discretion and my lips may preserve knowledge. Godly discretion defers anger and gives me patience; it enables me to overlook an offense.

Father, You are my God and my Teacher; You instruct me in discretion.

All this comes from You, the Lord Almighty. You are wonderful in counsel and magnificent in wisdom. Praise the Lord!

In Jesus' name I pray, amen.

Scripture References

Proverbs 1:4	Proverbs 19:11
Proverbs 2:11 NIV	Proverbs 19:11 NIV
Proverbs 3:21-26 NIV	Isaiah 28:26
Proverbs 5:1,2 NIV	Isaiah 28:29 NIV

To Display Integrity

Father, when You test my heart, may You be
pleased with my honesty. In everything I do, may I set
an example by doing what is good.

In my place of business may I show integrity, seriousness and soundness of speech that cannot be
condemned, so that those who oppose me may be
ashamed because they have nothing bad to say about
me. I purpose to manage, as David did, with integrity
of heart; with skillful hands he led the people.

Father, I thank You that the integrity of the
upright guides me. May I be blameless in Your sight so
that I wll receive a good inheritance. Let it be said of
me by all men, "We know you are a person of integrity
and that you teach the way of God in accordance with
the truth."

Judge me, O Lord, according to my righteousness, according to my integrity, O Most High, and
make me secure and guard me in Your righteousness.

In my integrity You uphold me and set me in Your presence forever.

In Jesus' name I pray, amen.

Scripture References

1 Chronicles 29:17 NIV	Matthew 22:16 NIV
Titus 2:7,8 NIV	Psalm 7:8 NIV
Psalm 78:12 NIV	Proverbs 13:5 NIV
Proverbs 11:3 NIV	Psalm 41:12 NIV
Proverbs 28:10 NIV	

To Go Forth in Peace

Father, I will guard my heart; and Your peace, which transcends all understanding, will guard my heart and mind. I choose to think on good things.

Because I love life and desire to see many good days, I keep my tongue from evil and my lips from speaking lies. I turn from evil and do good; I seek peace and pursue it. In my heart I have planned my course, and I look to You, Lord, to determine my steps.

I keep myself free from the love of money, and I am content with what I have, because You have said, "Never will I leave you; never will I forsake you." So I say with confidence, "The Lord is my Helper; I will not be afraid. What can man do to me?"

Surely goodness and mercy shall follow me today and all the days of my life, in the name of Jesus.

Lord, Your peace will act as umpire [continually] in my heart and will settle with finality all my decisions. You will keep me in perfect peace, Father, for my mind is stayed on You.

In Jesus' name I pray, amen.

Scripture References

Proverbs 4:23 NIV	Hebrews 13:5,6 NIV
Philippians 4:7,8 NIV	Psalm 23:6
Psalm 34:12-14 NIV	Colossians 3:15 AMP
Proverbs 16:9 NIV	Isaiah 26:3

To Exercise Humility

DEVOTIONAL READING

If you have any encouragement from being united with Christ, if any comfort from his love, if any fellowship with the Spirit, if any tenderness and compassion, then make my joy complete by being like-minded, having the same love, being one in spirit and purpose. Do nothing out of selfish ambition or vain conceit, but in humility consider others better than yourselves. Each of you should look not only to your own interests, but also to the interests of others.

Your attitude should be the same as that of Christ Jesus: who, being in very nature God, did not consider equality with God something to be grasped, but made himself nothing, taking the very nature of a servant, being made in human likeness. And being found in appearance as a man, he humbled himself and became obedient to death—even death on a cross! Therefore God exalted him to the highest place and gave him the name that is above every name, that at the name of Jesus every knee should bow, in heaven and on earth and under the earth, and every tongue confess that Jesus Christ is Lord, to the glory of God the Father.

Philippians 2:1-11 NIV

PRAYER

Father, I choose to clothe myself in humility and to receive Your grace as I humble myself before Your mighty hand. I expect a life of victory and awesome deeds because my actions are done on behalf of a spirit humbly submitted to Your truth and righteousness.

Allow my thoughts and actions to be pure, just and right. May I adjust my life so that I will know and understand the surety of Your plan for me.

Father, allow me to test my own actions, so that I can have appropriate self-esteem, without comparing myself to somebody else. The security of Your guidance will allow me to carry my own load with energy and confidence.

I desire to listen carefully and hear what is being said to me. I incline my ear to wisdom and apply my heart to understanding and insight.

Father, I know and confess that humility and the fear of the Lord bring wealth and honor and life. Therefore, as one of Your chosen people, holy and dearly loved, I clothe myself with compassion, kindness, humility, gentleness and patience. I bear with others and forgive whatever grievances I may have against anyone. I forgive as You forgave me. And over all these virtues I put on love, which binds them all together in perfect unity. I let the peace of Christ rule in my heart, and I am thankful.

Father, may Your will be done on earth in my life as it is in heaven.

In Jesus' name, I pray. Amen.

Scripture References

1 Peter 5:5 NIV	Proverbs 2:2
Psalm 45:4 NIV	Proverbs 22:4 NIV
Galatians 6:4,5 NIV	Colossians 3:12-15 NIV
Proverbs 18:12,13 NIV	Matthew 6:10 NIV

To Control the Tongue

Father, I commit to turn from idle words and foolishly talking things that are contrary to my true desire for myself and toward others. Your Word says that the tongue defiles, that it sets on fire the course of nature, that it is set on fire of hell.

In the name of Jesus, I am determined to take control of my tongue.

I am determined that hell will not set my tongue on fire. I renounce, reject and repent of every word that has ever proceeded out of my mouth against You, Lord, and Your operation. I cancel its power and dedicate my mouth to speak excellent things and right things. My mouth shall utter truth.

Father, I attend to Your words; I consent and submit to Your sayings. I will not let them depart from my sight; I keep them in the center of my heart, for they are life to me and to those to whom I speak— healing and health to all our flesh. I keep and guard

my heart with all vigilance and above all that I guard,
for out of it flow the springs of life. I put away from
me false and dishonest speech, and willful and contrary
talk I put far from me. My eyes look right on [with
fixed purpose], and my gaze is straight before me. I
guard my mouth and my heart with all diligence. I
refuse to give Satan any place in me.

Father, Your words are top priority to me. They
are spirit and life. I let Your Word dwell in me richly
in all wisdom. Your ability is released within me by the
words of my mouth; therefore, I speak forth Your
words. They are alive and working in me because You
are alive and working in me. So I can boldly say that
my words are words of faith, words of power, words of
love and words of life. They produce good things in
my life and in the lives of others. Because I choose
Your words for my lips, I choose Your will for my life,
and I go forth in the power of those words to perform
them in Jesus' name. Amen.

Scripture References

Matthew 12:36	Proverbs 4:20-25 AMP
Ephesians 5:4 NIV	Proverbs 21:23
2 Timothy 2:16 NIV	Ephesians 4:27
James 3:6	John 6:63
Proverbs 8:6,7	Colossians 3:16

To Dedicate a Business to God

In the name of Jesus, I proclaim that my purpose in establishing this business to which You have called me is to glorify You, Jehovah God. Today, I choose to set my mind and my sights on the [rich, eternal treasures] and joys of heaven, where Jesus sits beside You in the place of honor and power. Heaven fills my thoughts; worry about earthly things will not consume my time. I give You first place in my life (and in my business) and make a commitment to live as You want me to live, by the power of the Holy Spirit.

Thank You for working in me, that I might do Your will and act according to Your good purpose. I commit myself to carry out my responsibilities without complaining or arguing, so that I may become blameless and pure, a child of God, without fault in a crooked and depraved generation, in which I shine like a star in the universe, as I hold out the Word of life, in order that I may boast on the day of Christ that I did not run or labor for nothing.

With all that is within me I dedicate and consecrate this business to You, expressing my love to You. I embrace Your Word, hiding it in my heart, that I might not sin against You. For the whole world system, based as it is on the desires of men, the greedy ambitions and the glamour of all that they think splendid, is not derived from You at all, but from the world itself. The world and all its passionate desires will one day disappear. But the person who is following Your will is part of the permanent and cannot die.

Blessed be Your glorious name forever; let the whole earth be filled with Your glory. Amen and amen!

Scripture References

Colossians 3:1,2 AMP	Psalm 119:11
Matthew 6:33	1 John 2:15-17 PHILLIPS
Acts 1:8	Psalm 72:19 AMP
Philippians 2:13-16 NIV	

To Operate a Business as an Outreach

Father, You watch over Your Word to perform it. I desire to live so that my life reflects Jesus. Thank You for the wisdom that I need to promote Christ in this place of business. It is my desire that others will see my good works and glorify my Father in heaven.

Grant me the grace to live in harmony with myself, my family, employees, customers, vendors and suppliers as well as the general public. If possible, as far as it depends on me, I purpose to live at peace with everyone.

Thank You for sending the Holy Spirit to help all of us in this business to operate as one. Our peace, harmony and unity will be a testimony to the world that You have sent Jesus. May we be brought to complete unity to let the world know that You sent Jesus and that You love them even as You love Him.

Father, You have made me an agent of reconciliation; You have commissioned me with the message of reconciliation. I am now Christ's ambassador, as though You were appealing directly to others through me. For Christ's sake I beg others, "Make your peace with God. Now is the 'acceptable time'; this very day is the 'day of salvation.'"

Use this business as an evangelistic outreach to those who do not know You. As an able minister of the new covenant—a living epistle read by all men—I ask You for the wisdom to know how to present salvation to those who do not know You.

I will acknowledge the Lord Jesus Christ in all my ways, thanking Him for acknowledging me before You. I declare and decree on the authority of Your Word that I am salt and light. I am ready to give a quiet and reverent answer to anyone who wants a reason for the hope that is within me.

In Jesus' name I pray, amen.

Scripture References

Jeremiah 1:12 AMP

Matthew 5:16

Romans 12:18 AMP

John 14:16 AMP

John 17:21-24 NIV

2 Corinthians 5:18-21 PHILLIPS

2 Corinthians 6:2 PHILLIPS

2 Corinthians 3:6 AMP

2 Corinthians 3:2

Matthew 10:32

Matthew 5:13,14 AMP

1 Peter 3:15 PHILLIPS

To Make Tithes and Contributions

Father, You have entrusted to me the vision for this company, and I acknowledge You in all that I do. Your Word states, Be sure to set aside a tenth of all that your fields produce each year…so that you may learn to revere the Lord your God always (Deut. 14:22,23 NIV).

Thank You for the Holy Spirit, Who teaches me to revere. You. I love and worship You in spirit and in truth, bringing the tithe into the storehouse, that there may be food in Your house. Thank You for opening the windows of heaven and pouring out a blessing, that there shall not be room enough to receive it.

I purpose to be a faithful steward over that which You have provided. Thank You for giving me seed for sowing. It is a blessing and the rejoicing of my heart to support the gospel and bless others, in the name of Jesus.

As an outward expression of my heart commit-ment to You, I honor You with my substance, with the firstfruits of all my produce (increase and profit); then my barns will be filled to overflowing, and my vats will brim over with new wine.

Jesus is my Lord and my High Priest, and I bring to Him the firstfruits of the income of my business and worship You, the Lord my God, with them.

In Jesus' name I pray. Amen.

Scripture References

Proverbs 3:6

John 16:7-15 NIV

John 4:24

Malachi 3:10 NIV

Malachi 3:10

1 Corinthians 4:2

2 Corinthians 9:10

Proverbs 3:9

Proverbs 3:10 NIV

Hebrews 4:14 NIV

Deuteronomy 26:2-11 NIV

To Honor God in Business Dealings

Father, You are love, and I desire to be an imitator of You, that Your life may be manifested this day to my employees.

Thank You for wise counsel, for giving me ears to hear and for helping me to analyze all that I say and do for the good and betterment of my staff. Help me to speak truly, deal truly and live truly in harmony with You, myself and my co-laborers. In all my ways I acknowledge You, and You direct my ways.

Because I commit to You the decisions that I am responsible for making, You cause my thoughts to become agreeable to Your will and so my plans shall be established and succeed. Thank You for the courage to say no when it is necessary for the good of this company, and in keeping with Your plan and purpose for it.

We are an interdependent people—mutually dependent one upon the other. Each department operates in harmony and agreement—not [merely] concerned with its own interests, but also with the interests of others.

As an example to my employees, I commit to do to others what I would have them do to me. It is my desire to walk uprightly before You; therefore, I consider, direct and establish my way with the confidence of integrity.

You are my confidence, and You keep my foot from being snared. Your love is shed abroad in my heart so that I love my neighbor as myself.

In Jesus' name I pray, amen.

Scripture References

1 John 4:8

Ephesians 5:1 NIV

Ephesians 4:15 AMP

Proverbs 3:6

Proverbs 16:3 AMP

Philippians 2:4 AMP

Matthew 7:12 NIV

Proverbs 3:26 NIV

Romans 5:5

MISSION STATEMENT
Word Ministries, Inc.

To motivate individuals to spiritual growth

and emotional wholeness,

encouraging them to become more deeply

and intimately acquainted

with the Father God

as they pray prayers that avail much.

About the Author

Germaine Griffin Copeland, founder and president of Word Ministries, Inc., is the author of the *Prayers That Avail Much* family of books. Her writings provide scriptural prayer instruction to help you pray effectively for those things that concern you and your family and for other prayer assignments. Her teaching on prayer, the personal growth of the intercessor, emotional healing and related subjects have brought understanding, hope, healing and liberty to the discouraged and emotionally wounded. She is a woman of prayer and praise whose highest form of worship is the study of God's Word. Her greatest desire is to know God.

Word Ministries, Inc. is a prayer and teaching ministry. Germaine believes that God has called her to teach the practical application of the Word of Truth for successful, victorious living. After years of searching diligently for truth and trying again and again to come out of depression, she decided that she was a mistake. Out of the depths of despair she called upon the name of the Lord, and the light of God's presence invaded the room where she was sitting.

It was in that moment that she experienced the warmth of God's love; old things passed away and she felt brand new. She discovered a motivation for living—life had purpose. Living in the presence of God she has found unconditional love and acceptance, healing for crippled emotions, contentment that overcomes depression, peace in the midst of adverse circumstances and grace for developing healthy relationships. The ongoing process of transformation evolved into praying for others, and the prayer of intercession became her prayer focus.

Germaine is the daughter of Reverend A.H. "Buck" Griffin and the late Donnis Brock Griffin. She and her husband, Everette, have four children, seven grandchildren and four great-grandchildren. Germaine and Everette reside in Sandy Springs, a suburb of Atlanta, Georgia.

Word Ministries' offices are located in Historic Roswell, 38 Sloan Street, Roswell, Georgia 30075. Telephone: 770-518-1065.

You may contact
Word Ministries
by writing:

Word Ministries, Inc.
38 Sloan Street
Roswell, Georgia 30075
or calling 770-518-1065

www.prayers.org

*Please include
your prayer requests
and comments when you write.*

Other Books by Germaine Copeland

The Road God Walks

Prayers That Avail Much® Journal

Prayers That Avail Much® Commemorative Gift Edition

Prayers That Avail Much® Commemorative Leather Edition

Prayers That Avail Much® for Business Professionals

Prayers That Avail Much®—Volume 1

Prayers That Avail Much®—Volume 1
(Pocket Size)

Prayers That Avail Much®—Volume 2

Prayers That Avail Much®—Volume 2
(Pocket Size)

Prayers That Avail Much®—Volume 3

Prayers That Avail Much®—Volume 3
(Pocket Size)

Prayers That Avail Much® for Men

Prayers That Avail Much® for Women

Prayers That Avail Much® for Mothers
(Clothbound)

Prayers That Avail Much® for Mothers
(Pocket Size)

Prayers That Avail Much® for Teens

WWJD Prayers That Avail Much® for Students

Prayers That Avail Much® for Kids

Prayers That Avail Much® for Kids—Book 2

Oraciones Con Poder—Prayers That Avail Much®
(Spanish Edition)

Additional copies of this book are
available from your local bookstore

Harrison House
Tulsa, OK 74153

Prayer of Salvation

A born-again, committed relationship with God is the key to the victorious life. Jesus, the Son of God laid down His life and rose again so that we could spend eternity with Him in heaven and experience His absolute best on earth. The Bible says, **"For God so loved the world, that he gave his only begotten Son, that whosoever believeth in him should not perish, but have everlasting life"** (John 3:16).

It is the will of God that everyone receive eternal salvation. The way to receive this salvation is to call upon the name of Jesus and confess Him as your Lord. The Bible says, **"That if thou shalt confess with thy mouth the Lord Jesus, and shalt believe in thine heart that God hath raised him from the dead, thou shalt be saved. For whosoever shall call upon the name of the Lord shall be saved"** (Romans 10:9-10,13).

Jesus has given salvation, healing, and countless benefits to all who call upon His name. These benefits can be yours if you receive Him into your heart by praying this prayer:

> *Heavenly Father, I come to You admitting that I am a sinner. Right now, I choose to turn away from sin, and I ask You to cleanse me of all unrighteousness. I believe that Your Son, Jesus died on the cross to take away my sins. I also believe that He rose again from the dead so that I might be justified and made righteous through faith in Him. I call upon the name of Jesus Christ to be the Savior and Lord of my life. Jesus, I choose to follow You, and ask that You fill me with the power of the Holy Spirit. I declare that right now, I am a born-again child of God. I am free from sin, and full of the righteousness of God. I am saved in Jesus' name, Amen.*

If you have prayed this prayer to receive Jesus Christ as your Savior, or if this book has changed your life, we would like to hear from you. Please write us at:

Harrison House Publishers
P.O. Box 35035
Tulsa, Oklahoma 74153

You can also visit us on the web at
www.harrisonhouse.com

The Harrison House Vision

Proclaiming the truth and the power

Of the Gospel of Jesus Christ

With excellence;

Challenging Christians to

Live victoriously,

Grow spiritually,

Know God intimately.